A SUSSEX GUIDE

A DICTIONARY OF THE SUSSEX DIALECT

THE REVEREND W.D. PARISH

A DICTIONARY OF THE SUSSEX DIALECT & COLLECTION OF PROVINCIALISMS IN USE IN THE COUNTY OF SUSSEX
FIRST PUBLISHED IN THE YEAR 1875
BY THE REVEREND W.D. PARISH OF SELMESTON

INTRODUCED BY
LYNNE TRUSS

SNAKE RIVER PRESS

SNAKE RIVER PRESS

Book No 16
Books about Sussex for the enthusiast

Published in 2008 by
SNAKE RIVER PRESS
South Downs Way, Alfriston, Sussex BN26 5XW
www.snakeriverpress.co.uk

ISBN 978-1-906022-15-0

This book was conceived, designed and produced by
SNAKE RIVER PRESS

Copyright © Snake River Press Limited 2008
Text © The Reverend W. D. Parish & Lynne Truss

All rights reserved. No part of this book may be reproduced
in any form without written permission from the publisher.

The publishers and authors have done their best to ensure
the accuracy and currency of all information at the date of preparation.
Readers who intend to rely on the information to undertake any activity
should check the current accuracy. The publishers and authors accept
no responsibility for any loss, injury or inconvenience sustained by the
reader as a result of information or advice contained in this book.

ART DIRECTOR & PUBLISHER *Peter Bridgewater*
EDITORIAL DIRECTOR *Viv Croot*
EDITOR *Rob Yarham*
PAGE MAKEUP *Richard Constable & Chris Morris*
CONSULTANT *Lorraine Harrison*

This book is typeset in Perpetua & Gill Sans,
two fonts designed by Eric Gill

Printed and bound in China

DEDICATION

To my dear friends at Much Ado Books in Alfriston

CONTENTS

A DICTIONARY OF THE SUSSEX DIALECT & COLLECTION OF PROVINCIALISMS IN USE IN THE COUNTY OF SUSSEX
FIRST PUBLISHED IN THE YEAR 1875
BY THE REVEREND W.D. PARISH OF SELMESTON

PART ONE

INTRODUCTION

BY

LYNNE TRUSS

6

PART TWO

A DICTIONARY

OF THE

SUSSEX DIALECT

AND

COLLECTION OF PROVINCIALISMS

IN USE IN THE

COUNTY OF SUSSEX

BY

REV. W.D. PARISH

VICAR OF SELMESTON, SUSSEX

INTRODUCTION

> Mellors: *'Appen yer'd better 'ave this key an' Ah min fend for t'bods some other road.'*
> Lady Chatterley: *'Why don't you speak English?'*
> **LADY CHATTERLEY'S LOVER**, D.H. LAWRENCE, 1928

In 1924, the rural novelist Sheila Kaye-Smith rather beautifully illustrated her fears for the future of Sussex dialect. How would three generations from the same Sussex household respond verbally today, she asked, to the question of whether a storm was coming? Well, let's start with 'Grandfather', born perhaps in the 1860s, and accustomed to country ways. 'Surelye, fur de ships' tails is all to wind'ard,' the old man would observe, sagely, in pure bucolic vernacular, possibly chewing on a piece of grass and wearing a big white smock. Representing the next generation down would be 'Father', who had received a state education. Efficiently tapping his barometer, and speaking in standard English, 'Father' would offer the opinion: 'Well, it may be, for the glass is low.' Finally, and most worryingly, it would be the turn of 'Sonny', a child reared in a period of unstoppable 'Londonisation'. What do you think, Sonny: is there a storm coming? And in the universal cockney, 'Not half!' would be Sonny's depressingly cheerful reply.

Naturally, this 'Not half!' business was not music to the ears of Sheila Kaye-Smith. She was writing a new preface to John Coker Egerton's classic *Sussex Folk and Sussex Ways* (first published in 1884), and her tone was generally wistful. Sussex in the early 1920s was fast losing its character, as far as she was concerned; and in particular it was losing its language. The teaching of standard English in schools had a lot to answer for; on top of which, of course, greater mobility (and World War I) had exploded the isolation that preserves a community dialect. 'Sonny' hadn't got so far as to say 'Not Arf' yet, she wrote – 'but that is surely coming.' Little did she know, but the time was also fast approaching when a large number of people living in Sussex would be clueless about its traditional words, and deaf to its traditional pronunciations. In *Wunt Be Druv: A Salute to Sussex Dialect* (2006), the broadcaster David Arscott tells the story of a 'foreigner' (person from outside Sussex) asking a Sussex man in vain to help him find a 'Mister Pocock of Alciston', and repeating the question umpteen times before a third party intervened and pointed out that the chap busily denying all knowledge of Mr Pocock of Alciston actually was Mr Pocock of Alciston. Pocock was not abashed in the slightest. 'Why, you should ha' axed fur Mus Palk of Ahson!' he objected. Nowadays, of course, if a Sussex person refers to a town called Heffel, he will be quickly corrected, 'Oh, you mean Heathfield,' as if he's some kind of idiot.

W. D. Parish's wonderful *A Dictionary of the Sussex Dialect* was first published in 1875, 50 years before Sheila Kaye-Smith's all-too-prescient lament. No one said 'Not half!' yet in Sussex; or not, at least, when the Reverend Parish was in earshot with his pencil poised. Born in 1833, and appointed vicar of Selmeston (pronounced Simpson) when he was 30 years old, Parish was an accomplished educator and archaeologist whose only cause for resentment in life (or so I'm guessing) concerned his terrible disappointment at the font. Given that his father rejoiced in the fabulous, dashing name of Woodbine, how must 'W. D.' have felt to receive such prosaic christian names as 'William' and 'Douglas'? Sir Woodbine Parish, judging from the barest facts of his life, resembled a larger-than-life character from *Vanity Fair*: a Fellow of the Royal Society, he was an energetic diplomat and naturalist who distinguished himself in several large-scale contexts: by discovering the fossils of dinosaurs; by establishing British relations with the countries of South America; and by incidentally being the hand that penned the treaty of 1815 bringing an end to the Napoleonic wars.

Did he also give his name to a brand of cigarette? It is not impossible. Did he have a big fine twirly moustache? I have no idea, but I somehow can't imagine him without one. By contrast, Sir Woodbine's son, educated at Charterhouse and Trinity College, Oxford, is more of a George Eliot kind of chap, the stillness of his waters being (surely) a reliable indication of their depth. He led a far quieter life than his father, certainly, untouched by global politics, but it was a life of great usefulness nevertheless. All who speak of him seem to have affection for him – and no one has ever said a bad word about this, his most famous book. Inheriting his father's dual compulsion for digging things up and writing things down, he chaired the Sussex Archaeological Society, and (monumentally) edited the *Sussex Doomsday*. However, his greatest achievement of strenuous unearthing and meticulous recording is this invaluable, illuminating dictionary.

I must confess that, for me, the idea of any rural dialect has always been somewhat contaminated by Stella Gibbons and Rambling Sid Rumpo, so it may be best to get those obstacles to seriousness out of the way here and now. Like many people of my generation (and older) I grew up cheering for Rambling Sid on the BBC's *Round the Horne* ('Hello, me dearios!'), especially when he went a-rummaging in his ganderbag for a gladsome ditty to bend our ear-os with. Sung with the proper folk-revivalist's nasal twang by Kenneth Williams, most of his songs went to the tune of 'Oh My Darling Clementine'. For example:

> *Vain she was and like a grusset,*
> *Though her ganderparts were fine,*
> *But she sneered at his cordwangle*
> *As it hung upon the line.*

The exponential milking of innuendo from 'cordwangle', 'moulie' and 'gander' was absolutely shameless, but there was a general metropolitan sending-up of preposterously obscure country sayings at work, there, too. Every time you heard a line from Rambling Sid like, 'The fox be away with the goose and the fly be on the termutt,' you'd laugh partly because there were people in the world who said things that didn't begin to make sense.

Thirty years before *Round the Horne*, however, Stella Gibbons had paved the way for Rambling Sid's vernacular nonsense with her brilliant comic novel *Cold Comfort Farm* (1932), a book that just gets more and more remarkable the more one knows about it. Gibbons's clever device was to insert Flora Poste – a modern young woman with fixed views about happiness and common sense – into the kind of doomy Sussex fictional milieu made popular by writers such as Sheila Kaye-Smith (from whom we have already heard). Kaye-Smith's novels, which included *Sussex Gorse* (1916) and *The Tramping Methodist* (1922), were part of a somewhat turgid literary movement that exasperated the young Gibbons, not least for what she saw as its reliance on dialect to confer specious gravitas on quite ordinary stories. For *Cold Comfort Farm*, therefore, Gibbons invented such a perfectly satiric substitute Sussex idiom ('The cows be as barren as come-ask-it') that it was my first instinct, on seeing Parish's *Dictionary*, to check whether 'sukebind', 'middock', 'cowdle', 'mommet', 'capsy', 'a-mollocking' and 'scranlet' were historically authentic after all. 'I ha' scranleted two hundred furrows come five o'clock down in the bute,' one of the farmers says to Flora, leaving her clueless how to respond. Should she say, 'Oh, how too sickening for you?' or respond with a congratulatory 'Atta boy'? In the end she manages to say, 'Did you?' in 'a bright, interested voice', and seems to get away with it.

What makes Parish's *Dictionary* such a delight is, partly, that he compiled it before lexicography had quite found out what its full duties were. He could therefore ignore a lot of the dull and thankless work that would fall to the workers on the *Oxford English Dictionary*, for example, especially when it came to the always tricky business of determining where words had come from in the first place. The English Dialect Society was already in existence, but was sternly instructing its members to 'abstain from etymology' – which is probably, come to think of it, a recipe for sanity in any life, not just a lexicographer's. As he explains in his introduction, Parish at first resented this ruling. A man who goes to all the bother of collecting a word ought, surely, to be allowed to take first guess at its origins?

Yet the merest paddling in the shallows of etymology reveal how dangerous it is for the amateur, and one has to congratulate Parish for the highly sensible caution he adopted in the end. John Coker Egerton – vicar of Burwash contemporaneously with Parish at Selmeston – records in his *Sussex Folk and Sussex Ways* one ingenious local explanation for the name of his adopted village: that when the Romans landed at Pevensey in the first century BC they had a dog with them called 'Bur' who got a bit coated with Sussex clay as the army marched inland. And, yes, you've guessed it! 'Burwash' marks the spot . . . . . where Bur had a wash! Hence the name, you see! The fact that everyone called the village 'Berrish', and that it had been recorded as 'Borwese' in the time of Henry III, did nothing to undermine this confident attribution, apparently. But one can't help wondering: how did the inventor of this explanation account for the absence of other villages – 'Burwoof', 'Burwag-a-tail', 'Burchase-a-stick' – likewise marking key dramatic moments in good old Bur's noteworthy progress across the county?

There is nothing so daft, obviously, in Parish's *Dictionary*, but he rightly draws attention to the way Sussex dialect reflected so directly some of its intimate contact with invading forces from earliest times. Evidently in 1875 it was current in Sussex dialect to say, 'What a peter-grievous child you are! Whatever is the matter?' or 'We're all of a dishabill.' Parish ventures, not unreasonably, that 'peter-grievous' comes directly from the French *petit grief*, and 'dishabill' from *déshabiller*. Asking someone to speak up, a Sussex person in the east of the county might say, 'Quiddy? I didn't hear what you said.' And it's a fair assumption that 'quiddy' comes from '*Que dis-tu?*' although it's possible that 'quoth-ee?' might come into it, too. Meanwhile many terms from Old English were still in use in Sussex: 'maxon' for manure heap; 'mew' for seagull. Parish explains that Sussex shrimps were called 'pandles' from the Latin word *pandulus*, because the Romans landing at Pevensey (the ones with or without the dog) particularly liked the shrimps there.

Several points of interest will strike any peruser of this dictionary. For example, some of the terms are now familiar in standard English, which means either that they were already more common or widespread than Parish knew (and that he'd merely led a sheltered life), or that some of the 'Londonisation' process worked reciprocally, taking local dialect words into the mainstream. I am certainly not qualified to say which is the case, but it is still pleasant to speculate that a huffy, shirty, grizzling and lippy nipper in Sussex in 1875 who was also dog-tired and peaky but proper partial to a bit of maundering and passing the time of day would be perfectly at home in a standard slang sentence of today. Kaye-Smith, back in 1924, remarked that Sussex dialect had a strong affinity

INTRODUCTION

with 'real English as spoken in America', and there is evidence for that, too, in Parish's *Dictionary*. An American visitor would have been happy with 'coney' for rabbit, for example; or 'fall' for autumn; or 'moonshine' for smuggled spirits. 'Caterwise', meaning diagonally, may have a French origin (from *quartiers?*), but must surely connect with the American term 'catty-corners' for which British English has no equivalent.

What everyone wants from a book like this, of course, is funny, apparently meaningless, dialect exclamations like 'Fegs!' or 'Geemeny!' or, rather touchingly, 'Rabbits!' But what is more interesting (and tragic, of course) is that we have lost very expressive terms for which no decent substitute has ever come along. I love the term 'print moonlight' for clear moonlight (presumably clear enough to read by). To 'spannel' meant to tread mud into the house, in the manner of a dog (or spaniel). The clawing ritual performed by cats before they settle was called 'quilting' or 'making bread'. A thin, puny person was called 'windshaken'. A good friend, who stood by you through the lean times, was simply a 'bread-and-cheese friend'. A beverage consisting of beer, eggs and brandy was called 'Huckle-my-buff' – and I ask you: could such a hearty buff-huckling concoction possibly have been called anything else?

You can browse this book for hours, and you can argue with it, if you like. There are some expressions that hardly qualify as dialect, in a sense, being more like a garbled version of standard English. 'Dunnamuch' for 'don't know how much' is just legitimised elision, surely? 'Crownation' for coronation or 'brown-crisis' for bronchitis is just regular ignorance (like President George W. Bush saying 'nucular' for nuclear). Parish is very funny on Sussex folk not being generally able to distinguish between fairies and pharisees (but, being a vicar, he doesn't explore the rather interesting ramifications this must have had for their grasp of the gospel story). But when these people said 'ingenurious', were they perhaps deliberately combining the meanings of 'ingenious' and 'injurious', to describe a person who was exceptionally clever at hurting people? 'Ingenurious' is a truly indispensable word, once you've heard it. I know quite a few people who are ingenurious, but I never previously had the vocabulary to describe them.

One notices, above all, however, two big categories of dialect words in this book. First, all the local names for birds, bugs, beasts and plants (sukebind not being among them), and then all the words that point to a way of life – like the 'spanelling' I've already mentioned, which takes you straight into a lowly cottage with 'gurt' big muddy boot-prints appearing all over a recently-washed floor. The nature words are the ones you could never guess: 'rabbit's meat' would imply lettuce to me, or possibly the ferny stuff on the tops of carrots, but in fact 'rabbit's meat' was wild parsley. Weasels were 'futtices' or 'kimes', and a buttercup was a 'crow's foot'. A sparrow was a 'hedge-pick' or a 'hedge-mike'. Ground ivy was 'lion's mouth'. As you are beginning to guess, I could go on and on.

Of course, as a modern reader, one has urgent questions about the status of virtually every item of information in this dictionary. How widespread was each usage, for example? Did Parish hear these words from a hundred people, or just one or two (who might have been deliberately winding him up, of course; inventing 'huckle-my-buff' on the spot, just to test his gullibility)? Were some of the words already obsolete? What was the method of collection? Parish specifies which parts of the county the words come from (west, middle and east) but admits that he can't begin to identify which words are exclusive to Sussex speakers, hence his careful wording in the title about dialect that is 'in use in the County of Sussex'. Then there are further questions, such as: where are the juicy rude words for private parts, lustful feelings, sexual congress, adultery, everyday copulation with animals and so forth? There surely hasn't been censorship at work here? And personally, I'd like one small clarification: when Parish defined 'fagot' as a 'good-for-nothing girl', what did he mean, exactly? I ask because my father (born in London in 1922) addressed me as 'Fagot' (or 'Faggot') pretty well constantly when I was a small child, but he never explained where he got the word from or what on earth he was driving at.

Parish is not the only hero in the recording of Sussex dialect. The work is not over yet, either. On a BBC website, I recently found a lovely audio clip of the much-loved Brighton-based folk singer Shirley Collins talking about one of her favourite songs, *The Outlandish Knight*. An elderly Sussex woman had once told her she had rejected the advances of a young man on account of him being 'outlandish', and what this meant, apparently, was that he came from a village three miles away. But what all historians of Sussex speech since the 19th century have in common is an immense debt to W. D. Parish for the monumental work he did single-handedly 130 years ago. In the original edition of the *Dictionary*, published by Farncombe & Co in Lewes, perforated blank pages were included at the back of the volume, for keen readers to tear out and use if they wished to contribute additional words or usages to the project Parish had started. With some regret I have to report that the 1875 copy I have in front of me has all the blank pages still attached, which shows that even 130 years ago, people were a bit lazy about this kind of thing, and perfectly happy to let the dear old 'Vicar of Simpson' carry on doing all the donkey work.

Ask three generations today, anywhere in the south of England, whether there's a storm coming, and I think you might find a 'Londonisation' beyond Sheila Kaye-Smith's most harrowing nightmares. 'Oo you talking to?' says the grandfather. 'Oo wants to know?' asks the father, with fists raised. 'Wha'ever,' drawls the son. When I moved to Brighton in the early 1990s from South London I had the strange – but quite reassuring – sensation that I hadn't moved anywhere at all. I certainly didn't need to adapt my accent, or tune my ear. All my friends pronounce 'Herstmonceux' the way it's written, and have never heard of 'Horse-munzez'. When we say 'Let's go to Seaford' all the emphasis goes on the first syllable ('Sea-fud'), no matter how many times we're told that (in poetic, metrical terms) it's a spondee, with equal stress on both parts of the word. How many people say 'Chalvington' in preference to 'Charnton'? Well, all the people who actually want to be universally understood, obviously.

But this should not mean we aren't fascinated by the dialect that existed such a short time ago. Parish recorded the living speech of 'our kind-hearted old-fashioned Sussex folk, many of whom I number among my dearest friends' partly because he guessed it was already facing extinction, but mainly because he admired it. Whereas many dictionaries are redolent of book dust, lamp-oil and halitosis, this one conjures up a fresh, outdoor scene of a dog-collared man with a notebook talking to real, flesh-and-blood people (who are also, of course, incredibly tired and muddy), against a backdrop of shadows scudding across the Downs. No 'harmless drudge' definition pertains to Parish as a lexicographer. Read his book by print moonlight. Nibble on a stalk of rabbit's-meat while you're about it, and sip some huckle-my-buff. What you will discover is that Parish – a true, bread-and-cheese friend of the historic Sussex dialect if ever there was one – brings to this work a remarkable air of amusement, amazement and joy.

LYNNE TRUSS

Works mentioned
- JOHN COKER EGERTON: *Sussex Folk and Sussex Ways* (ed Henry Wace), Country Books, 2005
- DAVID ARSCOTT: *Wunt be Druv: A Salute to the Sussex Dialect*, Countryside Books, 2006
- STELLA GIBBONS: *Cold Comfort Farm*, Penguin, 2005

DICTIONARY OF
THE SUSSEX DIALECT

A DICTIONARY

OF THE

SUSSEX DIALECT

AND

COLLECTION OF PROVINCIALISMS

IN USE IN THE

COUNTY OF SUSSEX.

BY

REV. W. D. PARISH,

VICAR OF SELMESTON, SUSSEX.

SECOND EDITION.

LEWES:
FARNCOMBE & CO.

1875.

PREFACE.

THE march of education must sooner or later trample down and stamp out anything like distinctive provincial dialect in England; but when this result shall have been effected, much that is really valuable will be lost to our language, unless an effort is promptly made to collect and record words which, together with the ideas which first rendered them necessary, are rapidly falling into disuse.

Although in all such collections there will be a large proportion of words and phrases which are mere curiosities of expression, utterly useless to the science of language, yet there will remain a considerable number well worthy of being retained, and if possible revived.

Every year new words are being imported into the English language and gradually coming into general use amongst us. Too many of these are selected from the ghastly compounds of illiterate advertizers, and many more are of the most offensive type of slang—the sweepings of the music-hall, the leavings of the prize-ring and the worst specimens of Americanisms, selected to the exclusion of many good old English words which are to this day more frequently used in the United States of America than in our own country.

The English Dialect Society, which has lately been formed, will soon become the centre of a very valuable influence, by encouraging and uniting many word-collectors who have been quietly working for some time past in different parts of the country, and by giving a right direction to their labours.

To the Rev. W. W. Skeat, as the representative of that Society, I owe more than I am able to express for the guidance that he has given me, and the pains that he has taken to render this work as free as possible from imperfections. Without his assistance I could never have presented it to the reader in the form it now assumes.

Professor Bosworth also, although busily engaged (in his 87th year) in bringing out a new quarto Anglo-Saxon dictionary, found time to encourage me in my work, and set me in the right track by correcting the first pages of my proof. To him and many others my best thanks are due. Such a work could never have been done single-handed, and volunteers have come forward on all sides to help me.

The Rev. W. de St. Croix, late editor of the Sussex Archæological Society's Collections, has for many years given me valuable assistance. Miss Bessie C. Curteis, of Leasam, near Rye, has contributed at least 200 words, with conversational illustrations and legends from the East Sussex district. The Rev. J. C. Egerton, of Burwash, has also placed at my disposal his collection of upwards of 100 words in use in his section of the county; and when I add that the Rev. C. Swainson has helped me in my folk-lore, and Mr. James Britten, of the British Museum, has corrected my botanical definitions, the reader will understand how much kindly effort has been made to render my work successful, and how little its success (if it shall be attained) is due to myself.

W. D. PARISH.

LIST OF AUTHORITIES.

W. Durrant Cooper's Sussex Glossary.

Halliwell's Dictionary of Archaic and Provincial Words.

W. Holloway's General Dictionary of Provincialisms.

Bosworth's Anglo-Saxon Dictionary.

Sussex Archæological Collections.

Ayscough's Shakespeare.

Brand's Popular Antiquities.

R. Chambers' Book of Days.

Notes and Queries.

M. A. Lower, Contributions to Literature, &c., &c.

Professor Leo's Treatise on the Local Nomenclature of the Anglo-Saxons.

Stratmann's Old English Dictionary.

Wedgwood's Dictionary of English Etymology.

Ray's Collection of Local Words.

Bosham Manor Customs, and the Old Books of the Manor of Arundel (kindly lent by R. G. Raper, Esq.)

Various Inventories of Farm and Household Goods of the Last Three Centuries.

THE SUSSEX DIALECT.

IN almost every establishment in the country there is to be found some old groom, or gardener, bailiff, or factotum, whose odd expressions and quaint sayings and apparently outlandish words afford a never-failing source of amusement to the older as well as to the younger members of the household, who are not aware that many of the words and expressions which raise the laugh are purer specimens of the English language than the words which are used to tell the story in which they are introduced.

Every schoolboy home for the holidays at Christmas knows that the London cabman who drives him to the Theatre accentuates the word much more classically than the young gentleman who sits inside, who, if he had the audacity to pronounce Theatron with a short *a* in his next construe at school, would send a shudder through the Form amid which he would soon find himself in a lower place. So it is with our Sussex words; they sound strange to ears that are not accustomed to them; and by some persons they may be supposed to be mere slang expressions, not worthy of attention; but when they are examined, many of them will be found to be derived from the purest sources of our language, and to contain in themselves a clear reflection of the history of the county in which they are used.

Every page of this dictionary will show how distinctly the British, Roman, Saxon and Norman elements are to be traced in the words in every day use among our labouring people, who retain among them many of the oldest forms of old words which although they have long ago become obsolete among their superiors in education, are nevertheless still worthy of our respect and attention. Like the old coins which he so often turns up with his plough, the words of the Sussex labourer bear a clear stamp of days long past and gone and tell a story of their own.

The fact that I have lived for several years in a village spelt Selmeston and pronounced Simpson; within reach of Brighthelmston, pronounced Brighton, and next to the village of Chalvington, called Charnton, will, I think, be considered sufficient excuse for the direction my studies have taken. My daily intercourse with persons speaking the purest Sussex dialect has enabled me to add from time to time many fresh words to the excellent list published by Mr. Durrant Cooper in his "Glossary" (which must always be the guide book for all who take an interest in the subject); and when I found that I had added as many as a thousand words to those which he had already published, I thought I might venture to take the next step forward in making known the Sussex dialect among Sussex people by the publication of this book. I had called it a dictionary of the Sussex dialect before I was aware that my friend Mr. M. A. Lower had stated in an article published in the Sussex Archæological Collections that there is no such thing as a Sussex dialect at all. I should be sorry to appear to set up my opinion in opposition to one whose authority on all matters connected with the antiquities of our county is so generally recognized; but I am sure that he will allow me the use of the word to indicate a form of speech, which in words and pronunciation is strictly defined by geographical boundaries, and frequently proves completely unintelligible to strangers who hear it for the first time.

So far as a distinct collection of words can be called a dialect, it may be said that there are three dialects in use in the County of Sussex, the East Sussex, Mid Sussex and West Sussex; and it will be observed that I have marked this distinction in the following pages by affixing to most of the words the initial of the district in which they are used. But besides these, there are many words which, as far as I can ascertain, are common to the whole county, and to these no distinctive letter is annexed.

I should (roughly) define the East Sussex district as the part of the county lying east of a line drawn northward from Hastings; the West Sussex district would be bounded by a line running northward from Shoreham; and the Mid Sussex district would, of course, be found between the two. I must request the reader to bear in mind these geographical distinctions, because few persons except word-collectors are acquainted with provincial expressions beyond their own district; and without this explanation it might be supposed that many words which occur in my list are not Sussex words at all.

The sources from which our Sussex words are derived will naturally have a special interest for many of my readers. All who collect or study strange words are anxious to know where they come from; and I confess that I was much surprised when I found that one of the first pieces of advice which was circulated among the members of the English Dialect Society was to abstain from etymology. It seemed to me that to encourage people to collect words, and at the same time to forbid them to attempt to give their derivations, was very like presenting a boy with a pair of skates and then desiring him on no account to go upon the ice. I little knew how treacherous was the element from which this humane society warns us off, till I was myself involved in its dangers, and only just rescued by the untiring efforts of the secretary, Mr. Skeat, from the consequences of rashness which might have been fatal to the success of my work.

Etymology is for many reasons surrounded with dangers and difficulties, not only on account of the prevalence and perpetuation of erroneous derivations already existing, on the authority of persons who knew nothing whatever of the subject, but also because there are so few works published on the subject which are reliable.

Besides this, every amateur etymologist, who fancies he has made a fresh discovery, is led to make a series of wild shots at derivations, forgetting that it is the *history* of a word, and *not the similarity* of it to another in form or sound, which determines the source from which it is derived; so one mistake leads to others, and the confusion becomes every day worse confounded.

Still, I am aware that after all that can be said, word collectors will never be satisfied with merely collecting without deriving, and many of them will be at first inclined to resent any restriction of their liberties; therefore I hope that the English Dialect Society will take an early opportunity of buoying the dangerous channels of etymology, and give a few clear and distinct directions whereby we may be able to steer a safe course within certain defined limits.

The dialect of the Sussex people has been affected by the geographical position and the history of the county. It may be traced chiefly to Anglo-Saxon, Old Dutch, Old Welsh (or British), with a dash of 14th century French, and a little Scandinavian, the latter due to the sea-coast, which has for many generations invited hosts of friendly invaders to our shores, and has twice witnessed the landing of armies destined to influence the history and language of the whole country.

When the Roman legions landed on our coast they left an evidence of their appreciation of the Pevensey shrimps, which remains to this day in the word *pandle*, derived from the Latin *pandalus*, which is in constant use in this part of the county.

The arrival of the Normans, and the foundation of their large monastic establishments marks a very distinct phase in the history of our vocabulary.

But it will be observed that most of our words now in common use, denoting agricultural and domestic implements, are either to be traced to an Anglo-Saxon derivation, or actually retain their original Anglo-Saxon names in all purity of spelling and pronunciation. From this source also nearly all the Sussex surnames and names of villages and farms (noticed in the Appendix) are derived. Nor must I forget to remark that when the Sussex peasant speaks of the sun as *she*, he uses an expression which clearly asserts his German origin.

As might be expected, many words are due to our proximity to the coast. The Sussex fishermen, in their constant intercourse with their Dutch and French brethren, although finding much difficulty in parleying to their satisfaction, have nevertheless for many generations adapted and introduced so many foreign words into common use among themselves, that their vocabulary is almost worthy of being called a fourth branch of the dialect.

Other circumstances, too, have tended to the increase of the French influence. Between 1562 and 1572 no less than 1,400 refugees from France settled themselves in Sussex, and many of their names may be still traced among our labouring people in the eastern division of the county. Besides this, the establishments of French prisoners in later times, and the custom which still prevails, though not so much as it did, of shopkeepers and townsfolk exchanging children with French families in order that each might learn enough of the other's language to be useful in after life, has kept the French element alive amongst us, and accounts for the existence of many words which are not so much derived from as positive corruptions of modern French.

But besides those words in the Sussex dialect which are really valuable as having been derived from authentic sources, there are a great many which are very puzzling to the etymologist, from the fact of their having been either actually invented without any reference to the laws of language, or adapted and corrupted from other words. A Sussex man has a great facility for inventing words. If he has any difficulty in expressing himself, he has no hesitation about forming a word for the occasion. This he does on the phonetic principle (if it can be said to be done on any principle at all), and as he prefers a long word, the result of his invention is generally very curious indeed; and whether or not the word serves the purpose for which it was intended, it is sure to be caught up by some one else, and, especially if it is a long one, is very soon incorporated among the words available for general use in the village.

There are also many words which are used to convey meanings totally different to their original intention. These may be called words of substitution. They are introduced in this way,—a person hears a word which he does not quite understand; he does not take the trouble to ascertain either the meaning or pronunciation of it, but he uses a word *something like it*. This is specially the case with the names of complaints, such as will be found incidentally mentioned in some of the illustrations which I have given of the use of Sussex words, as, for instance, brown-crisis for bronchitis, and rebellious for bilious, &c. The names of any but the most common trees and shrubs are also strangely perverted. A friend of mine had a gardener who persisted in calling an acacia the Circassian, and after much pains had been taken to point out the mistake, never got nearer than calling it the cash-tree. I have heard chrysanthemums called Christy anthems, and China asters Chaney oysters; but that was by the same man who also once enquired how I made out with "them Scotch-Chaney fowls" of mine.

It is also surprising how little trouble people will take to ascertain correctly even the names of their neighbours, and I know an instance of a man who lost sight of his own name altogether, from having been accustomed for many years to hear it mispronounced. But this in a great measure is to be attributed to the fact that a musical ear is very rarely found among Sussex people, a defect which is remarkably shown not only in the monotonous tunes to which their old songs are sung, but also in the songs themselves, which are almost entirely devoid of rhythm.

The Sussex pronunciation is, generally speaking, broad and rather drawling. It is difficult to say why certain long words are abbreviated, or why certain short words are expanded. In some names of places every syllable, and even every letter, is made the most of—as Eäst Hoädlye for East Hoathly—while others, like the name of my own village, are abruptly curtailed from three syllables to two by the most ruthless excision.

As far as I can reduce the pronunciation of the Sussex people to anything like a system it is this,—

a before double *d* becomes *ar;* whereby ladder and adder are pronounced larder and arder.

a before double *l* is pronounced like *o;* fallow and tallow become foller and toller.

a before *t* is expanded into *ea;* rate, mate, plate, gate, are pronounced reät, meät, pleät, geät.

a before *ct* becomes *e;* as satisfection for satisfaction.

e before *ct* becomes *a;* and affection, effect and neglect are pronounced affaction, effact and neglact.

Double *e* is pronounced as *i* in such words as sheep, week, called ship and wick; and the sound of double *e* follows the same rule in fild for field.

Having pronounced *ee* as *i*, the Sussex people in the most impartial manner pronounce *i* as *ee*, and thus mice, hive, dive, become meece, heeve and deeve.

i becomes *e* in pet for pit, spet for spit, and similar words.

io and *oi* change places respectively; and violet and violent become voilet and voilent, while boiled and spoiled are bioled and spioled.

o before *n* is expanded into *oa* in such words as pony, dont, bone; which are pronounced poäny, doänt, and boän.

o before *r* is pronounced as *a;* as carn and marning, for corn and morning.

o also becomes *a* in such words as rad, crass, and crap, for rod, cross, and crop.

ou is elongated into *aou* in words like hound, pound and mound; pronounced haound, paound and maound.

The final *ow*, as in many other counties, is pronounced *er,* as foller for fallow.

The peculiarities with regard to the pronunciation of consonants are not so numerous as those of the vowels, but they are very decided and seem to admit of less variation.

Double *t* is always pronounced as *d;* as liddle for little, &c., and the *th* is invariably *d;* thus the becomes *de;* and these, them, theirs—dese, dem and deres.

d in its turn is occasionally changed into *th;* as in fother for fodder.

The final *ps* in such words as wasp, clasp, and hasp are reversed to wapse, clapse and hapse.

Words ending in *st* have the addition of a syllable in the possessive case and the plural, and instead of saying "that some little birds had built their nests near the posts of Mr. West's gate," a Sussex boy would say "the birds had built their nestes near the postes of Mr. Westes' gate."

Thus I have tried as nearly as possible to define the rules of Sussex pronunciation—there are so many exceptions to all the rules that they can scarcely be called rules at all; but with regard to one letter a rule can be given which admits of no exception. The letter *h* is never by any chance used in its right place; and any one who has ever attempted to teach a Sussex child to read, must be convinced that nothing short of a surgical operation could ever introduce a correct pronunciation of the aspirate into his system.

I may here state that I have endeavoured to spell the words in this dictionary as nearly as possible as I have heard them pronounced; but in the examples of Sussex conversation, &c., I have not attempted to follow out the exact pronunciation of the shorter words, because if I had done so, I should probably have rendered them incomprehensible to many of my readers and tiresome to all.

It now remains for me to state the principle upon which I have selected certain words for my dictionary, to the exclusion of others which have been given in the glossaries of Ray, Cooper, Halliwell and Holloway, as Sussex words.

I had to choose from,—

1. Words found only in some parts of Sussex;
2. Words found in Sussex only; and
3. Words found in Sussex, and also in other Counties.

With respect to the first two classes of words there was no question beyond that of identification, and as regards their identity as being actually in use in the county, I may say that I have by myself, or upon the authority of friends on whom I can rely, personally identified almost all of the eighteen hundred words which will be found in this collection. But the reader will easily understand that my chief difficulty has been in dealing with provincialisms unquestionably used in Sussex, but also in such common use elsewhere as apparently to deprive them of a distinctive character. The rule of my selection has been to include any provincial word not likely to have been adopted from a book, which I found in constant use among people who, as far as I could ascertain, had never been out of the county; and lest any of my readers should be inclined to complain of the admission of many words not distinctly belonging to Sussex, I have guarded myself in the title of the book I offer to their perusal, which is not only a dictionary of the Sussex dialect, but also a collection of provincialisms in use in the County of Sussex.

I have also endeavoured to illustrate the use of the words by specimens of conversation, most of which are taken from the life verbatim, and will serve to indicate some phases of character and thought which find frequent expression among our people. When the opportunity has occurred I have added examples of folk lore and proverbial philosophy which are rapidly becoming obsolete, and if not recorded may in another generation be entirely forgotten. Many of them point to superstitions, which are remarkable from the very fact they should exist at all in the presence of our advanced civilization, and many more are connected with old customs already passed away.

I hope that they may at least serve the purpose of inducing some persons to look through the pages of my book, who would otherwise have taken no interest in a mere collection of words; and perhaps when they see how many interesting points may be elicited from closer intercourse with their poorer neighbours, they may be persuaded to become in their turn collectors of old words and stories of the past.

I am convinced that there are many more words yet to be recorded, and I hope that some of my readers will send me materials for a larger dictionary of the Sussex dialect, which I hope some day to be able to complete. I have little doubt of finding many persons ready to help me in this respect, for I have already received much assistance from persons who were strangers to me till they saw my name in connection with this publication; and even up to the last moment, while my work has been in the hands of the printers, several words have been sent me too late to find a place in the alphabetical list. I have, therefore, requested the publishers to add at the end of each volume a few blank pages, so perforated as to be easily detached without injury to the book, in the hope that such persons as are willing to help me, may write down and forward to me any words not hitherto published which may come under their notice; adding always the name of the locality in which they are used, their pronunciation if it seems necessary, and any proverb or anecdote which may add to their interest.

In making this announcement I acknowledge the imperfection of my own work. Such a work must of necessity be tentative and imperfect, but such as it is I offer it to the kind perusal of all who are interested in the old-world ideas and language of our kind-hearted old-fashioned Sussex folk, many of whom I number among my dearest friends.

A DICTIONARY

OF

THE SUSSEX DIALECT.

Note.—The letters *e*, *m*, or *w*, after a word, indicate that it is used in East, Mid or West Sussex. By East is meant the extreme East of the County. The words marked with an asterisk are those which I have not myself been able to identify, but are given on the authority of the glossaries of Durrant Cooper, Halliwell, or Holloway.

A.

A. The prefixed a-, as used in the Sussex dialect, generally adds some slight force or intensity, and is retained in such words as a-dry, a-lost, a-nigh, &c.

It is also almost invariably used with the participle; as, "I am a-going as soon as I can."

A-BEAR. [*A-béran*, Ang. Sax.] An old form of bear, in the sense of endure or like. Used in the negative, "I never could a-bear that chap."

A-BED. In bed.

ABIDE. [*Abídan*, Ang. Sax.] To endure. Used with the negative in the same way as a-bear.

ABOUTEN, *e*. [*Abútan*, Ang. Sax.] Just on the point of having done anything.

Always used with a past tense; as, "I was abouten going out, when Master Noakes he happened along, and he kep' me."

The syllable en is more frequently omitted in Sussex; as, "My knife wants sharping."

ABROAD, *m*. In all directions; all about.

ABUSEFUL, *m.* Abusive.

ABUSEFULLY, *m.* In an abusive manner.
"As my missus was a-going home a Saddaday night, she met Master Chawbery a-coming out of the Red Lion, and he treated her most abusefully, and threw abroad all her shop-goods. He's a man as aint no account at all aint Master Chawbery."

ACCOUNT. Esteem; reputation.
"The Princes both make high account of you."
—*Richard III.*, Act iii. sc. 2.

ACHE, *e.* To tire. "I am afraid you'll ache waiting so long."
To long for anything. "Nancy just will be pleased, she has ached after a dole I don't know the time when."

ADIN. [Corruption of Within.]
The initial w is mostly omitted in Sussex; and th is always pronounced as d; thus, the wood becomes de 'ood; and within idin or adin.

ADLE. [Ang. Sax., *ádl.*] Pronounced ardle. Stupid.
"He's an adle-headed fellow."

ADLE, *e.* Slightly unwell.
"My little girl seemed rather adle this morning, so I kep' her at home from school."

ADONE. [Have done.] Leave off.
I am told on good authority that when a Sussex damsel says "Oh! do adone," she means you to go on; but when she says "Adone-do," you must leave off immediately.

ADRY. Thirsty.

AFEARD. [*Afõered*, Ang. Sax.] Afraid.
"Hal, art thou not horribly affeared?"
—1 *Henry IV.*, Act ii. sc. 4.

AGARVES, *m.* May berries.

AGIN. [*Agen*, Ang. Sax.] Near to; against.
"He lived up agin the Church, and died about forty yeere agoo."

AGOO. Ago.

AGREEABLE. Acquiescent; consenting.
"They asked me if I'd come in and have a cup o' tea, and I was quite agreeable;" meaning that he accepted the invitation.

Agwain. Going.

Along-of. On account of.
> "Along of her it was that we met here so strangely."
> —*Cymbeline*, Act v. sc. 5.

This expression is often expanded into all-along-of, and even, all-through-along-on-account-of; as "Master Piper he lost his life all-through-along-on-account-of drink."

All-on, *m.* Incessantly.
"He kept all-on making a noise."

All-one. All the same; as,
"Well, 'tis all one whether ye do or whether ye doänt."

Allow. To give as an opinion.
"As I was agwaine down the street, I ses to Master Nappet ses I, what d'ye think of this here job down at the blacksmith's? I ses, and Master Nappet he allowed that it was amost too bad!"

Alltsinit, *m.* [All that's in it.] Merely.

Amendment, *m.* Manure.
"You go down to the ten-acre field, and spread that amendment abroad, and peck up them ammut-castes."

Ammuts, *m.* Emmets; ants.

Ammut-castès. Emmet-castes; ant-hills.
This form of plural is invariably retained in words ending with st, as postes, nestes. The reduplicated plural is also not unfrequently used; and a Sussex man would see nothing absurd in saying,—
> "I saw the ghostesses,
> Sitting on the postesses,
> Eating of their toastesses,
> And fighting with their fistesses."

Amost. Almost.

Amper.* A flaw or fault in linen or woollen cloth.

Ampery, *m.* [*Ampre*, Ang. Sax., a flaw.] Beginning to decay, especially applied to cheese.

Ampery. Weak; unhealthy.

Ampre-ang.* A decayed tooth.

Ancley, *m.* }
Ancliff, *e.* } Ankle.

Ancliff-bone. In East Sussex, I have put out my ancliff-bone, is equivalent to I have sprained my ankle.

ANDIRONS. The ornamental irons on each side of the hearth in old fire-places, before grates were introduced. The andirons were sometimes made of superior metal, or gilt, and of very large dimensions.

> "Her andirons (I had forgot them) were two winking cupids of silver." —*Cymbeline*, Act ii. sc. 4.

ANEWST.* [*Neawest*, Ang. Sax.] Nigh; almost; near at hand.

ANIGH. Nigh; near.

AN. Of. "If you wants to be rid an him, you *lend* him a sixpence; I lay he'll never come anigh you no more."

ANYWHEN. At any time.

APPLETERRE.* [Apple and *terre*, French.] An orchard.

APPLETY, *e.* [Apple, and tye an enclosure.] An apple-loft, where the fruit is kept.

This word is used on the borders of Kent, in which county the word tye means an enclosure, whereas in Sussex it means an open common.

APSE. [*Æpse*, Ang. Sax.] An aspen tree.

ARDER. An adder. In Sussex the letters a and e are often pronounced as in French.

The country people say that an adder can never die till sunset. If it be cut to pieces, the bits will retain their vitality till the sun goes down. They also say that on the adder's belly will be found the words,—

> "If I could hear as well as see,
> No man in life could master me."

ARG, *m.* To argue; to wrangle.

"These chapelfolks always wants to arg."

ARGIFY, *m.* To signify; to import.

"I do'ant know as it argifies much whether I goos to-day or whether I goos to-morrow."

ARTER. [Corruption of After.]

ASHEN. Made of the wood of the ash.

ASLEW, *m.* Aslant.

ATWEEN. Between. Also used in the Eastern Counties.

ATWIXT. Betwixt.

AWHILE. For a time.

"We shan't have no gurt frostes yet awhile—not atwixt now and Christmas, very like."

AVISED, *e.* [*Aviser*, French.] Aware of. To know for a certainty.

"I'm well avised that John spent all his wages at the Barley-mow."

AUMRY, *e.* [*Aumoire*, Old French, a cupboard.]
or
AWMRY, *e.* A large chest.

"And when they had eaten, King Arthur made great clerks to come before him that they should chronicle the high adventures of the good knights; and all was made great books and put in almeries at Salisbury."
—*Sir Thomas Malory's Morte D'Artur.*

AXEY, *e.* The ague. A complaint which is very prevalent in many parts of Sussex. There is a different name for it in almost every district. In some places it is believed that it may be cured by the following charm, which, to be efficacious, must be written on a three-cornered piece of paper and worn round the neck till it drops off,—

"Ague, ague, I thee defy,
Three days shiver,
Three days shake,
Make me well for Jesus' sake!"

B.

BACKSTAYS, or BACKSTERS. Wide flat pieces of board, made like snow shoes, which are strapped on the feet and used by the fishermen in walking over the loose beach or soft mud on the seashore.

BACKTURNED, *m.*
and
BACKWENT, *m.* These words, which are evidently of Saxon construction, can only be explained by giving instances of their use. "He was backturned when I saw him," means "he was standing with his back to me." "I only saw him backwent," means "I only saw him as he was going away from me."

BAIT, *m.* Afternoon refreshment, with which strong beer is given, in the hay and harvest field.

BALDERDASH.[*] [Probably derived from Ang. Sax., *Baldwyrda*, a saucy jester.] Obscene conversation.

BALLET, *m.* A ballad.

Bannick, *m.* To beat.

"I'll give him a good bannicking if I catch him."

Barley-champer, *w.* An instrument for cutting off the beards of the barley.

Bark. To cough.

"I can't abear for my master to goo to church; for he keeps up such a barking, that nobody can't hear naun for him."

Barton, *m.* [*Bere-tún*, Ang. Sax., a court-yard.] The demesne lands of a manor. The manor house itself. More frequently the outhouses and yards.

Barway, *m.* A field-gate, made of bars or rails so fitted as to draw out from the posts.

Bat. [*Bâton*, French, a stick.] A rough walking-stick.

Batch. A quantity of bread baked at once without heating the oven afresh.

"How now, thou core of envy?
Thou crusty batch of nature, what's the news?"
—*Troilus and Cressida*, Act v. sc. 1.

Batfowler. One who takes birds at night with a large folding-net on long poles, called a batfowling net.

Gon: "You are gentlemen of brave metal; you would lift the moon out of her sphere, if she would continue in it five weeks without changing."
Seb: "We would so, and then go a batfowling."
—*Tempest*, Act ii. sc. 1.

Batter. [*Abattre*, French, to beat down.] A wall which diminishes upwards is said to batter.

Bavins. Brushwood faggots.

"The skipping king, he ambled up and down,
With shallow jesters and rash bavin wits,
Soon kindled, and soon burnt."
—1 *Henry IV.*, Act iii. sc. 2.

Bawl, *e.* To read aloud.

A mother said of a child who did not go to school on account of illness, "I keeps him to his book all the same, and his father likes to hear him bawl a bit in the evening."

Bay. A pond-head made up to a sufficient height to keep in store water.

Bay. A compartment of a barn. The space between the main beams of the roof: so that a barn crossed twice with beams is a barn of three bays.

"If this law hold in Vienna ten years, I'll rent the fairest house in it, after three-pence a bay." —*Measure for Measure*, Act iii. sc. 2.

BE. A common prefix to verbs, generally conveying a reflective and intensitive power, as be-smeared, be-muddled, be-spangled.

BEACH, *m.* Shingle brought from the sea-coast is always called beach, as opposed to the inland gravel.

BEAT THE DEVIL ROUND THE GOOSEBERRY-BUSH, *e.* To tell a long rigmarole story without much point.

> An old man at Rye said he did not think the new curate was much of a hand in the pulpit, he did beat the devil round the gooseberry-bush so.

BEAZLED, *m.* Completely tired out.

> "He comes home tired of an evening, but not beazled like boys who go to plough."

BECK. [*Becc*, Ang. Sax., a brook.] A rivulet.

BECK, *w.* [*Becca*, Ang. Sax., a pickaxe.] A mattock.

To BECK, is to use the beck or mattock.

BEDSTEDDLE. A bedstead.

BEEPOT. A beehive.

BEESKEP, *e.* [*Scep*, Ang. Sax., a basket.] A beehive, or the straw hackle placed over the hive to protect it.

> There is a superstition in the county, that if a piece of black crape is not put round the hive after a death in the family, the bees will die.

BEEVES, *m.* A corruption of Bee-hives; the i in the word hives being pronounced as in French.

> "Well, John, how are you going to make out this winter? Well, I reckon I shall have to make brooms and beeves."

BEEVER, *w.* Eleven o'clock luncheon.

BEGRIDGE, *m.* To grudge.

BEHITHER, *e.* On this side. It answers to beyond.

> "The fifty-first milestone stands behither the village, and the fifty-second beyond."

BEING. An abode; a lodging.

> " Return he cannot, nor
> Continue where he is: to shift his being,
> Is to exchange one misery for another."
> —*Cymbeline*, Act i. sc. 6.

BELEFT, *m.* Perfect of believe.

> "I never should have beleft that he'd have gone on belvering and swearing about as he did."

Belver, *m.* To make an angry disturbance.

Bench. A widow's bench is the share of the husband's estate which a woman enjoys besides her jointure.

Best, *m.* To get the better of anyone; to beat at any game.
"I bested him every time."

Bethered, *e.* Bed-ridden.
"Poor creature! She was bethered three years before she died."

Bethwine. The wild clematis.

Bettermost. Superior; above the average. Generally qualified by the word rather.
"The new people who have come to live down at the cottage seem rather bettermost sort of folks."

Bibler-catch, *w.* [*Bilboquet*, French.] The game of cup and ball.

Bide. [*Bídan*, Ang. Sax., to remain.] To wait; remain.
"If ye've got one you can run;
If ye've got two you may goo;
But if ye've got three
You must bide where you be."
—*Sussex Proverbial Advice to a Young Mother.*

Bind-days, *w.* Days on which the tenants of certain manors were bound to work for their lord.

Bine, *m.* The hop stalk which binds round the pole.

Biscuit. In Sussex the words biscuit and cake interchange their usual meaning. A plum biscuit, or a seed biscuit, means a plain cake made of either of these ingredients.

Bishop-Barnaby, *e.* The lady-bird.
In some parts of Sussex the lady-bird is called the lady-bug; in others, fly-golding, or God Almighty's cow, by which singular name it is also known in Spanish (Vaca de Dios). The children set the insect on their finger, and sing,—
"Bishop Bishop-Barnabee,
Tell me when my wedding shall be;
If it be to-morrow day,
Ope your wings and fly away."

Bitten, *m.* [*Bítende*, Ang. Sax., biting.] Inclined to bite.
"Mind that dog, he's terrible bitten."

Bittle, *w.* A wooden milk bowl.

Bittle-battle. The game of stoolball.

There is a tradition that this game was originally played by the milk-maids with their milking-stools, which they used for bats; but this word makes it more probable that the stool was the wicket, and that it was defended with the bittle, which would be called the bittle-bat; hence the word bittle-battle.

Blackeyed Susan, *m.* A well pudding, with plums or raisins in it.

Blame. A common substitute for a worse word.

"Blame ye! ye be always at something; be blamed if I doant give it yer one of these days."

Blanket-pudding, *m.* A long round pudding, made of flour and jam; sometimes called a bolster-pudding.

Bleat, *m.* Cold; cutting; applied to the wind.

Blobtit, *m.* A tell-tale.

Blunder, *m.* A noise as of something heavy falling.

"I heard a terrible blunder overhead."

Blunder. To make a noise.

Bluv, or **Bliv.** [Corruption of Believe.] "I bluv" is often used at the end of an assertion in the sense of "you may take my word for it," as, "'Taint agoing to rain to-day, I bluv."

Bly, *e.* [*Bleo,* Ang. Sax., hue.] A resemblance; a general likeness.

"I can see a bly of your father about you."

Bobbingneedle, *m.* A bodkin.

Boco, *e.* [*Beaucoup,* French, much.] A large quantity. This word is principally used by the fishermen.

Bodger. [Corruption of Badger.]

Boffle. A confusion or mistake.

"If you sends him of a errand he's purty sure to make a boffle of it."

Boke. [*Bealcian,* Ang. Sax.] To nauseate.

Bondland, *w.* [*Bonde-land,* is defined in Bosworth's Anglo-Saxon Dictionary as land held under restrictions.]

Used in Framfield and Mayfield for old cultivated or yard-lands, as distinguished from assart-lands, which were parts of forests cleared of wood and put into a state of cultivation, for which rents were paid under the name of assart-rents.

Book. The Bible is almost always spoken of by old people as the Book. Not many years ago the family Bible was the only book to be found in the cottages of the poor; now the frequent visits of the book-hawker have introduced a taste for reading into the remotest districts of the county, but still the Bible retains its title of the Book; and I was glad to hear a rough-looking carter boy say the other day, "I always read a bit of my Book before I goos to bed."

Boot-legs, *m.* Short gaiters, not reaching to the knee.

Boss. To throw.

Bostal, or Borstal. A pathway up a hill, generally a very steep one, and on the northern escarpment of the Downs; as the White Bostal near Alciston, the Ditchling Bostal, &c.

With respect to the derivation of this much-disputed word, Professor Bosworth has kindly given me the following:—Burg-stal,-stol, es; *m* [burg, beorg, beorh, a hill, stal a place, seat, dwelling.] A hill-seat, dwelling on a hill; sedes super collem vel clivum, Cot. 209. The name of places built on a hill, as Burstall in Suffolk, Borstall in Kent and Oxfordshire, &c.

Mr. Kemble (Sussex Archaeological Collection, vol. ii., p. 292) takes "the first word of the compound to be the Saxon word *beorh*, a hill or mountain, the passing of which into bor, is neither unusual nor surprising. The second word is not so easily determined. Were the word ever written borstill, Mr. K. should suggest the Saxon *stigel*, a stile or rising path; and beorh-stigel would be the hill-path or mountain-path. He does not know whether, in that branch of the West Saxon which prevailed in Sussex, 'steal' did signify a road or way; but it is not without probability that some of the Anglo-Saxon dialects might have justified that use of the term; for 'stealian' or 'stellan' does sometimes seem to be applied in the sense of 'going or leaping.'"

Bottom, *m.* A valley in the Downs.

Bottom, *w.* A reel of cotton.

Bouge, *m.* [*Bouge*, French.] A water cask.
    The round swelling part of a cask.

Bough-house, *m.* A private house allowed to be open at fairs for the sale of liquor.

An old person describing the glories of Selmeston fair, which has now been discontinued many years, said "There was all manner of booths and bough-houses."

In former times putting up boughs upon anything was an indication that it was to be sold, and a bush at the end of a pole was the badge of a country ale house; which gave rise to the proverb, "Good wine needs no bush," *i.e.*, nothing to point out where it is sold.

BOULDER-HEAD. A work against the sea, made up of small wooden stakes.

BOUT. A day's work.
"I shan't do it this bout," means, I shall not finish to-day.

BOZZLER, *m.* A parish constable; a sheriff's officer.

BRABAGIOUS, *e.* An adjective of reproach, the exact meaning of which is difficult to define; but it is generally considered available for use in a quarrelsome discussion between females. "You nasty brabagious creature."

It seems to combine the advantages of Mrs. Gamp's two principal epithets, bragian and bage.

BRAKE. The common fern. *Pteris aquilina.*
   "I'll run from thee and hide me in the brakes."
        —*Mid. Night's Dream*, Act ii. sc. 2.

BRAKE. A kneading trough.

BRANDS, or BRANDIRONS. Irons used for supporting the brands for burning wood in a wood fire.

BRAVE, *m.* [*Brave*, French.] Well in health.
"How are you, John?" "I'm bravely, thank you."

BRAVE, *m.* Prosperous.
"I have been making out bravely since you were last here."

BREACHY. Brackish, applied to water.

BREACHY. [*Brèche*, French, a breach.] A word applied to cattle which are wild and liable to break through the fences.

BREAD-AND-BUTTERS, *m.* [Compare, *Butter-brod*, German.] Pronounced brenbutters; slices of bread buttered; used in the same way as the French word *tartine*.

BREAD-AND-CHEESE-FRIEND, *e.* A true friend as distinguished from a cupboard-lover.
"He's a regular brencheese friend he is, not like a good many, always after what they can get."

BRICKS, *m.* The paved walk in front of a cottage, or paved path in a garden.
"I'm always pleased to see him a-coming up my bricks."

BRITT, *m.* [*Brytan*, Ang. Sax., to break.] To shatter like hops from being over-ripe.

BROACH, *w.* [*Broche*, French.] A spit.
> "Broached with the steely point of Clifford's lance."
> —III *Henry VI.*, Act ii. sc. 3.

BRONK, *m.* A disdainful toss of the head.
> "She didn't choose to see me, so she just gave a bronk and passed on."

BROOK, *m.* A water meadow.

BROOM-DASHER, *m*, BROOMSQUIRE, *w.* A dealer in faggots, brooms, &c.
The word dasher is also combined in haberdasher.

BROOM-CLISHER, *m.* [Clish, a bond.] A broom maker.

BROWN-BIRD, *m.* Thrush.

BRUFF, *e.* Rough; short in manners and speech.

BRUSS, *m.* [Compare French *Brusque*, blunt.] Proud; upstart.

BRUSTLES. [Variation of Bristles.]

BRUTTE, *e.* [*Brouter*, French, to nibble.] To browse or feed upon.

BRUTTLE. Always in Sussex used for brittle.

BUCKING, *m.* [*Buc*, Ang. Sax., a tub.] A washing of clothes.

BUD, *w.* A calf of the first year, so called because the horns then begin to appear or bud.

BUDDY, *w.* Stupid, in the same sense as the word calf is often used for a stupid fellow.

BUDGE, *w.* [*Bouge*, French.] A cask placed on wheels for carrying water. (See Bouge.)

BUDGE, *m.* [*Bouder*, French, to pout.] Grave; solemn.
> "He looked very budge when I asked him who stole the apples."

BUG. Any hard-winged insect.

BULLOCK, *m.* A fat beast of either sex.
I was very much astonished when I first heard a farmer say, "Yes, she's a purty cow, a very purty cow indeed, and one of these days she'll make a nice bullock."

BUMBLESOME, *m.* Hunched up; misfitting.

BUMBOO, *m.* A mysterious compound of spirituous liquors, under the influence of which, Mr. Turner, draper, of Easthoathly, made the following entry in his diary:—"1756, April 28th. I went down to Jones', where we drank one bowl of punch and two muggs of bumboo, and I came home again in liquor. Oh! with what horrors does it fill my heart to think I should be guilty of doing so, and on a Sunday too! Let me once more endeavour, never, no never, to be guilty of the same again."

BUNCH, *m.* A swelling.

"It came out in bunches all over me."

BUNGER, *m.* To do anything awkwardly.

BUNNY, *w.* A wooden or brick drain laid under a road or gateway to carry off the water; also called a cocker.

BUNT, *e.* To rock a cradle with the foot; to push or butt.

A bunt is described to me as a push with a knock in it, or a knock with a push in it.

"I'll give you a middlin' bunt prensley if you doänt keep still."

BUNTER, *m.* An old-fashioned machine for cleaning corn.

BURGH, *m.* [*Burg*, Ang. Sax.] A rising ground; a hillock. The term is frequently applied to the barrows or tumuli on the Downs.

BURNISH, *e.* To grow fat. The expression, "You burnish nicely," meaning, "You look well," is frequently used in East Sussex, and is meant as a compliment.

BUTTER-MY-WIG, *m.* A strong asseveration.

"No I wunt; butter my wig if I will!"

BY-THE-BYE, *e.* By chance.

"He come along one day by-the-bye, or else he hasn't been a-nigh me for the last ten years."

BYTHEN. By the time that.

"Bythen you've come back 'twill be coager-time."

BYSTE, *m.* A couch made up of two chairs for a child to sleep upon in the day-time.

BYSTE, *m.* To lie down in the day-time.

"I was quite took to (ashamed) to think you should have come in the other day and found me bysted, but I was quite entirely eat up with the rheumatics, and couldn't get about no hows."

C.

Cab.* [*Cabaler*, French, to plot.] A small number of persons secretly united in the performance of some undertaking.

Cadger. Not only a travelling beggar, but anyone given to begging is called by this name in Sussex.

Call out of Name, *m.* To call a person out of his name is not to give him his proper title.

"And then, what d'ye think he says? Why, he says 'ooman,' and I aint a-going to be called out of my name by such a fellow as him, I can promise him."

Call-over, *m.* To abuse.

"He come along here a cadging, and fancy he just did call me over, because I told him as I hadn't got naun to give him."

Callow, *m.* [*Calo*, Ang. Sax., bald.] Smooth; bare.

The woods are said to be getting callow when they are just beginning to bud out.

Camber, *e.* A harbour.

Winchilsea Castle, built to protect Rye harbour, is called Camber Castle.

Camsteery, *e.* A horse is said to be very camsteery when it does not go steadily.

In Northumberland the word means crazy.

Cant. To upset or let fall.

"The cart canted over and he was canted out into the road."

Cant. A corner of a field.

A haystack is said to be cut across in cants, and a field of wheat is divided into cants when it is partitioned out in slips for the reapers, each of whom takes one or more cants as his share of work.

Carfax. [*Carrefourgs*, Old French, crossways.] A place where four roads meet, as the Carfax at Horsham.

Carp-pie.* To eat carp-pie is to submit to another person's carping at your actions.

Catch Hot, *e.* To take a fever.

CATCH HURT, *m.* To meet with an accident. An old man once told me that he catched hurt at Chiddingly Church, meaning that he got married there.

CATERCROSS, *w.* Slanting.

CATERING, *m.* From corner to corner.

CATERWISE, *m.* Diagonally.

"If you goos caterwise across the field you'll find the stile."

CATS TAILS. The male blossom of hazel or willow.

CATTERNING. To go catterning is to go round begging for apples and beer for a festival on St. Catherine's Day, and singing,—

"Cattern' and Clemen' be here, here, here,
Give us your apples and give us your beer,
One for Peter,
Two for Paul,
Three for him who made us all;
Clemen' was a good man,
Cattern' was his mother;
Give us your best,
And not your worst,
And God will give your soul good rest."

CAVINGS, *w.* [*Ceaf,* Ang. Sax., chaff.] The short straws or ears which are raked off the corn when it is thrashed.

CAVING-RIDDLE, *w.* A sieve for cavings.

CERTAIN SURE, *e.* The superlative of certainly.

"I hope you are pretty well to-day. Certain sure, indeed!"

CHACKET, *m.* To cough.

CHANCE-BORN, *e.* An illegitimate child.

CHAMP, *w.* Firm; hard.

"The river has a champ bottom."

CHANGES. Shirts and shifts.

If you ask what a girl or boy stand most in need of on first going to service, you are sure to be told "changes." I have not got a change means, I have no linen.

The following inventory of the outfit of a girl going to service is taken from the account book of Selmeston parish, 1745:—"An account of Grace Barber's cloaths,—14 caps and moobs, 2 changes, one gown, 2 white hancerchifs, 3 coats, 2 spackol hancerchifs, one white apron, 2 other aprons."

CHAPEL-MASTER, *m.* A dissenting preacher.

CHARGER, *e.* A large platter or meat dish.

CHARM-STUFF, *e.* Ague medicine.

In Sussex, medicine is generally spoken of as *physical medicine*, but it is carefully distinguished from doctor's stuff, by which a tonic is meant.

The use of charms, especially in cases of ague or wounds, is still prevalent in the country; and the following charm is not unfrequently used for the cure of a burn. It must be repeated three times,—

> "Two Angels from the North,
> One brought fire, one brought frost:
> Out fire, in frost,
> In the name of the Father, the Son, and the Holy Ghost."

CHASTISE, *m.* To accuse.

"They've been chastising my boy of setting the faggot-stack a-fire."

CHAVISH, *e.* A chattering or prattling noise of many persons speaking together.

A noise made by a flock of birds.

CHECK, *m.* To reproach or taunt.

"He checked him of his cousin Tom (who had been sent to prison)."

CHEE, *e.* A hen-roost. Going to chee is going to roost.

CHEQUER, *w.* The service tree. *Pyrus torminalis.* The fruit is called chequers.

CHESS, *e.* A plaid.

"I brought a chess shawl for mother."

CHICK. In East Sussex used as the plural of chicken.

"I reckon you have got a good sight of chick here."

CHICKEN. In Mid-Sussex used as the plural of chick.

CHILL. To take off the extreme coldness from any beverage by placing it before the fire.

"I often gets my mistus to chill a drop of beer for me, when I comes home winter evenings."

CHIZZLE, *w.* Bran.

CHIZZLY, *e.* [*Ceosel*, Ang. Sax., sand.] Gritty; harsh and dry under the teeth.

CHOGS, *m.* The refuse cuttings of the hop plants when dressed in the spring before being polled.

CHOICE, *m.* Careful.

"He aint got but two brockyloes, but he's middlin' choice over them, I can tell ye."

CHOCK. To choke.

CHOCKLY, *m.* Choky; dry.

CHOPPER, *w.* A dried pig's face.

CHOW, *m.* To chew.

"The old cow's better this morning, she's up and chowing her quid."

CHUCKER, *m.* Cosily; to chucker oneself is to chuckle over anything.

CHUCKS, *m.* Large chips of wood.

CHUCKLE-HEADED. Stupid.

CHUFF, *m.* Churlish; surly.

"The old gentleman he went out to get a few chucks, and there they was, a sitting in the wood-house together jes' as chucker; and he was middlin' chuff about it, I bluv!"

CHURCH-BAWLED, or CHURCH-CRIED, *m.* Having the banns published in church.

The tradition in Sussex is that if a person goes to church to hear himself cried, his children will be born deaf and dumb.

CHURCH-LITTEN, *m.* [*Lictùn*, Ang. Sax., a burying-place.] A church-yard.

CLAM. [*Clam*, Ang. Sax., anything that holds or retains.] A rat-trap.

CLAPPER. The tongue.

"He hath a heart as sound as a bell, and his tongue is the clapper; for what his heart thinks his tongue speaks."
—*Much Ado About Nothing*, Act iii. sc. 2.

CLAVELS, *w.* The separate corns in an ear of wheat.

CLEAT, *e.* A piece of wood placed to prevent a door or gate from swinging backwards and forwards.

CLEAT-BOARDS, *w.* Mud pattens; broad flat pieces of board fastened on the shoes to enable a person to walk on the mud without sinking into it; much used by the eel-spearers at Chichester harbour and elsewhere.

CLEMMENING. Going round from house to house asking for apples and beer for St. Clement's Day.

In spite of a proclamation made at London, July 22, 1540, that "neither children should be decked ne go about upon St. Nicholas', St. Catherine, St. Clement, the Holy Innocents', and such-like days," the children in some parts of East Sussex still keep up the custom of catterning and clemmening, and the Sussex blacksmiths are particularly active in commemorating their patron saint; the anvils are fired with a loud explosion, and at least a half-holiday is kept. At Burwash, a few years ago, it was the custom to dress up a figure with a wig and beard and a pipe in his mouth, and set it up over the door of the inn where the blacksmiths feasted on St. Clement's day.

CLIM. To climb.

CLINKERS. Small bricks burnt very hard and used for paving. The hard refuse cinders from a forge fire.

CLISH, *m.* The bond or band by which heath or birch brooms are fastened.

CLITCH, *w.* A cluster.

CLOCKSMITH, *m.* A watchmaker.

"I be quite lost about time, I be; for I've been forced to send my watch in to the clocksmith. I couldn't make no sense of mending it myself; for I'd iled it and I'd biled it, and then I couldn't do more with it."

CLOGUE, *m.* To flatter.

CLOPPERS, or CLOG-BOOTS. Boots with wooden soles, worn by the fishermen on some parts of the coast.

CLOSE, *w.* A farmyard.

CLOVERLAY. [*Clæfer* and *leag*, Ang. Sax.] A field of clover which has been lately mown.

CLUCK, *m.* Out of spirits; slightly unwell. A hen is said to be cluck when she wants to sit.

CLUNG, *m.* Cold and damp.

The mown grass is spoken of as very clung after having been exposed to wet chilly weather, so that it has not hayed satisfactorily.

CLUTCH, *e.* Close; tightly.

"If you takes up a handful of the hay and holds it pretty clutch, you'll soon see 'taint fit to carry, for 'tis terr'ble clung."

CLUTCH, *w.* A brood of chickens or a covey of partridges.

CLUTTER-UP, *m.* To throw into confusion; to crowd.

COARSE, *e.* Rough; stormy; applied to weather.

COARSE, *e.* Childish.
"She is twelve years old, but she is so coarse for her years that you would not take her to be but ten."

COAST.* [*Coste,* Old French, a rib.] The ribs of cooked meat, particularly lamb.

COBBLE-STONES. Pebbles on the sea shore.

COCKER, *w.* A culvert; a drain under a road or gate.

COCKER-UP. To spoil; to gloss over with an air of truth.
"You see this here chap of hers he's cockered-up some story about having to goo away somewheres up into the sheeres; and I tell her she's no call to be so cluck over it; and for my part I dunno but what I be very glad an't, for he was a chap as was always a cokeing about the cupboards, and cogging her out of a Sunday."

CODDLE, *e.* To parboil.
Apples so cooked are called coddled-apples.

CODGER. A miser; a stingy old fellow.

COG, *m.* [*Cogger,* Old English, a trickster.] To entice.
"I cannot flatter, and speak fair,
Smile in men's faces, smooth, deceive, and cog."
—*Richard III.,* Act i. sc. 3.

COAGER, *m.* Luncheon. Called in some parts of the county an elevener, from the time at which it is generally taken by the labourers.

COAGER-CAKE. A plain cake is often baked as the coager cake, for the week's consumption.

COILERS. (See Quilers.)

COKE, *m.* [*Kijken,* Dutch, to peep about.] To pry about.

COLE.* Seakale.

COME. When such a time arrives.
"I shall be eighty-two come Ladytide."

COMMENCE, *m.* An affair; a job.
"Here's a pretty commence!"

COMP, *m.* [*Comp,* Ang. Sax.] A valley.
Some cottages in the parish of Beddingham are called by this name, from which also the name of the village of Compton is derived.

Coney, *m.* A rabbit.
> "There is no remedy: I must coney-catch,
> I must shift."
> —*Merry Wives of Windsor*, Act i. sc. 3.

Concerned in Liquor, *e.* Drunk.

This is one of the many expressions used in Sussex to avoid the word drunk. To have had a little beer, means to have had a great deal too much; to have half-a-pint otherwhile, means to be an habitual drunkard; to be none the better for what he had took, means to be much the worse; to be noways tossicated, implies abject helplessness. A Sussex man may be tight, or concerned in liquor, but drunk never!

In the village of Selmeston the blacksmith's shop is next door to the public-house. I have met numbers of people going up to the forge, but never one going to the Barley-mow.

Contrairy. [*Contraire*, French.] Disagreeable; obstinately self-willed.

A man describing his deceased wife, to whom he was really very much attached, said, "She was a very nice, pleasant 'ooman as long as no one didn't interrupt her, but if you had ever so few words with her, she'd be just as contrairy as ever was a hog."

Contraption, *m.* Contrivance; management.

A pedlar's pack is spoken of sometimes as his contraption.

Comb, *m.* An instrument used by thatchers.

Cooch-grass. [*Cwic*, Ang. Sax.] A coarse, bad species of grass, which grows very rapidly on arable land, and does much mischief by the long stringy roots which it throws out in great quantities.

Barnes says, with reference to this—Cooch, couch grass, quitch grass, creeping wheat grass, *Triticum repens*. Mr. Vernon suggests that it was originally quick grass, from its lively growth.

Coombe, or **Combe**, *m.* [*Cwm*, Welsh, a valley.] A hollow in the Downs.

This word is to be traced in the names of many Southdown villages and farms, such as Telscombe, Ashcombe, &c.

Coolthe, *e.* Coolness.
"I set the window open for coolthe."

Cop, *e.* To throw; to heap anything up.

Copson, *w.* A fence placed on the top of a small dam laid across a ditch for the purpose of keeping sheep from going over it.

Cord. A cord of wood is a pile of wood cut up for burning, 8ft. by 4ft. and 4ft. thick.

Cordbats, or Cordwood, *m.* Large pieces of wood, roots, &c., set up in stacks.

Core, *w.* [*Cœur*, French, heart.] The middle of a stack of hay which has been cut away all round.

Cotteril, *w.* A pothook; or a hook to hang spits on.

Cousins, *e.* To call cousins, is to be on intimate terms; but it is generally used in the negative, as, "She and I doänt call cousins at all."

Countable. A contraction of unaccountable.
"My mistus is countable ornary agin to-day."

Cracklings, *w.* Crisp cakes.

Crank, Cranky, *e.* Merry; cheerful; also drunk.

Crap, or Crapgrass. Ray-grass. *Lolium perenne.*

Cray-ring, *m.* The ring on the top of the long handle of a scythe into which the blade is fixed.

Crazy. Out of order; dilapidated. An old decayed building is said to be crazy.

Crazy-house. A lunatic asylum.

Creepers, *m.* Low pattens mounted on short iron stumps instead of rings.

Crip, or Crup. Crisp.

Crisscross [Christ's Cross], *m.* The alphabet; so called because in the old horn books it was preceded by a cross.

In the north of England a crisscross is the mark of a person who cannot write his name.

Crock, *e.* A smut or smudge.
"You have got a crock on your nose."

Crock. [*Crocca*, Ang. Sax., a pitcher.] An earthen vessel.
"Go to the end of the rainbow and you'll find a crock of gold." —*Sussex Proverb.*

The Bavarians have a similar proverb; but they say that the crock can only be found by one who was born on a Sunday, and that if such a person can find it and retain it in his possession, it will always contain three ducats.

Crock Butter, *m.* Salt butter, which in Sussex is usually potted down in brown earthenware crocks.

CROFT, *m.* [*Croft*, Ang. Sax., a small enclosed field.] A small piece of pasture land near to a house.

CROSS-WAYS. A place where four roads meet.

CROWNATION. Coronation.

"I was married the day the Crownation was, when there was a bullock roasted whole up at Furrel (Firle) Park. I doänt know as ever I eat anything so purty in all my life; but I never got no further than Furrel cross-ways all night, no more didn't a good many."

CROWSFOOT. The butter-cup. *Ranunculus bulbosus* and allied species.

CRUMMY. Fat; fleshy.

"He aint near so crummy as what he was afore he went to Lewes jail."

CRUTCHES, *e.* [*Cruche*, French, a pitcher.] Broken pieces of crockery.

CRY, *e.* Several dogs of all kinds.

"I knew it was Miss Jane, by reason she'd got the cry with her."

CUCKOO'S BREAD AND CHEESE TREE, *m.* The whitethorn.

"When the cuckoo comes to the bare thorn,
Sell your cow and buy your corn." —*Old Proverb.*

It is very remarkable that this name should be given to the whitethorn, as among all Aryan nations this tree is associated with the lightning, while the cuckoo is intimately connected with the lightning gods, Zeus and Thor.

CUCKOO-FAIR. Heathfield fair, held on April 14th. The tradition in East Sussex is that an old woman goes to Heathfield fair, and there lets the cuckoo out of a bag.

In Worcestershire the saying is that the cuckoo is never heard before Tenbury fair (April 21st), or after Pershore fair (June 26th).

With this may be compared the following German legend, given by Grimm in his "Deutsche Mythologie," p. 691:—
"Our Lord was one day passing a baker's shop, when, feeling hungry, He sent in one of His disciples to ask for a loaf; the baker refused it, but his wife, who with his six daughters was standing at a little distance, gave him the loaf secretly, for which good deed they were placed in heaven as seven stars—the Pleiades; but the baker was changed into a cuckoo, which sings from St. Tiburtius' Day (April 14) to St. John the Baptist's Day (June 24), that is, as long as the seven stars are visible."

A Dictionary of the Sussex Dialect.

CUCKOO GATE, *m.* A gate which shuts upon two posts which are connected with curved bars, so constructed that only one person can conveniently pass through at a time, and for this reason called in Hampshire a kissing-gate.

CULLS, or CULLERS, *m.* The inferior sheep of a flock, culled from the rest and offered for sale in a lot by themselves.

CULVER. A pigeon or dove. This name is retained in the name of a field at Selmeston, which is called the culver ake (the pigeon's oak).

CURIOUS, *e.* Unsteady; drunk.
"Doänt sit so curious when you're swinging, or you'll fall out."

CUSS. Surly; shrewish.

CUT YOUR STICK. Be off.
This expression is either simply equivalent to a recommendation to prepare a staff in readiness for a journey; or it may be connected with the old way of reckoning by notches or tallies on a stick, and so imply a settlement of accounts before departure.

CUTTY, *m.* A wren; also called a kitty.

D.

DAB. The sea-flounder.

DALLOP, *m.* A parcel of tea packed for smuggling, weighing from six to sixteen pounds.

DALLOP. A clumsy, shapeless lump of anything tumbled about in the hands.

DANG, or DANNEL. Substitutions for damn.

DAPPEN, *m.* By the time; or perhaps an abbreviation of "should it happen."
"Dappen I've done this job I'll come and lend yer a hand."

DARKS, *m.* A word used by sailors, but more particularly by smugglers, to signify those nights when the moon does not appear.
In former times, everyone in the agricultural districts of Sussex within reach of the coast was more or less connected

with smuggling. The labourer was always ready to help whenever the darks favoured "a run;" the farmer allowed his horses to be borrowed from his stable; the parson (certainly at Selmeston) expressed no surprise at finding tea and tubs buried in the churchyard vaults; the squire asked no questions; the excisemen compounded with the smugglers, and when a difficulty arose as to price, and hard blows where struck, the doctor bound up the wounds for nothing, and made no enquiry as to the dallops of tea or kegs of French brandy, which from time to time were found mysteriously deposited on his doorstep at daybreak.

DARLING, or DAWLIN, *m.* The smallest pig of a litter; an unhealthy child.

DEAD ALIVE. Dull; heavy; stupid.

DEAD HORSE, *e.* To work for a dead horse is to labour for wages already received, or to work out an old debt.

DEAL, *m.* The nipple of a sow.

DEARED. Deafened.

"I was amost deared, they made such a noise."

DEATH, *m.* Deaf. It is rather startling to be told that a person is afflicted with deathness.

DEE, and TO-DEE. Day, and to-day.

DEEDY. Clever; industrious.

DEEDILY, *e.* Earnestly.

"You was talking so deedily that I didn't like to interrupt you."

DEESE, *e.* A place where herrings are dried, now more generally called a herring-hang, from the fish being hung on sticks to dry.

DEEVE. Dive. The pronunciation of the i like that of the French i is very common in Sussex.

DENIAL, *m.* A hindrance. "His deathness is a great denial to him."

DENSHER PLOUGH, *m.* [Devonshire plough?] An instrument used for turf-cutting.

DENTICAL, *m.* Dainty.

"My master says that this here Prooshian (query, Persian?) cat what you gave me is a deal too dentical for a poor man's cat; he wants one as will catch the meece and keep herself."

A Dictionary of the Sussex Dialect.

DEVIL. This word scarcely ought to have a place in a dictionary of the Sussex dialect, for the country people are very careful indeed to avoid using it. The devil is always spoken of as *he*, with a special emphasis.

"In the Downs there's a golden calf buried; people know very well where it is—I could show you the place any day. Then why dóànt they dig it up? Oh, it is not allowed; *he* would not let them. Has anyone ever tried? Oh, yes, but it's never there when you look, *he* moves it away."

DEZZICK, *m*. A day's work.

"I aint done a dezzick for the last six months."

DICK. [*Dic*, Ang. Sax., a trench.] A ditch.

DIGHT. [*Dihtan*, Ang. Sax., to prepare.] To adorn; to dress. "She is gone upstairs to dight-up."

DIMSEL, *e*. A piece of stagnant water, larger than a pond and smaller than a lake.

DISH OF TONGUES. A scolding.

"He'll get a middlin' dish of tongues when his mistus comes to hear an't."

DISHABILL. [*Déshabillé*, French, an undress.] Disorder.

" My house is not fit for you to come in, for we're all of a dishabill."

DISHWASHER. The water-wagtail.

DISREMEMBER, *m*. To forget.

" I can't think of his name; I do disremember things so."

DISSIGHT, *m*. An unsightly object.

DOBBS, or MASTER DOBBS, *e*. A kind of brownie or house-fairy who does all sorts of work for members of the family. " Master Dobbs has been helping you," is a common expression to use to a person who has done more work than was expected.

DOBBIN. Sea-gravel mixed with sand.

DODDLE. To wag; tremble; walk infirmly.

DODDLISH. Infirm.

"Old Master Packlebury begins to get very doddlish."

DODDLEGRASS. *Briza media*, or quaking grass, called in the north "doddering dick."

DOG, *m*. An instrument used by thatchers.

DOGS. Small rests for the logs in the old open hearths, the top or ornamental part of which very often had the head of a dog on it.

Dog-tired. Completely wearied out.
> "Oh, master, master, I have watched so long
> That I am dog-weary."
> —*Taming of the Shrew*, Act iv. sc. 2.

Doles, *m.* The short handles on the snethe of a scythe.

Dole. [*Daél*, Ang. Sax., a portion.] Gifts; alms distributed on St. Thomas' day.

Doling, *e.* A fishing boat with two masts, each carrying a sprit-sail. Described in Boys' History of Sandwich as "Ships for the King's use furnished by the Cinque Ports."

Dollers. The people who go round gathering doles.

Dolphin. A fly which attacks the beans.

Done-over. Tired out; a transposition of over-done, in the same way as go-under is always used for undergo.

Doole. A conical lump of earth, about three feet in diameter at the base, and about two feet in height, raised to show the bounds of parishes or farms on the Downs.

Dosses, or Dorsels, *e.* Panniers in which fish are carried on horseback.

Dout, *e.* [Do out.] To extinguish the light of a candle.

Douters. Instruments like snuffers, used for extinguishing a candle without cutting the wick.

Dowels, *e.* Levels; low marshes in which the water lies in winter and wet seasons.

Down. Laid up by illness.
> "He's down with a bad attackt of brown crisis on the chest, leastways that's what the doctor calls it."

Down-bed. A bed on the floor.

Dozzle. A small quantity.
> "He came in so down-hearted that I couldn't be off from giving him a dozzle of victuals, and I told him if he could put up with a down-bed, he might stop all night."

Dracly-minute. Immediately.
> "Ye be to goo dracly-minute."

Draggle-tail. A slut.
> "Dame Durden kept five serving maids
> To carry the milking pail,
> *   *   *
> *   *   *
> 'Twas Doll and Bet and Sall and Kate,
> And Dorothy-draggle-tail."

DRAINING-SPOON, *w.* An iron tool used by drainers to take out the earth which crumbles down to the bottom of the cutting.

DRAUGHT. A drawing.
"There was a gentleman making a draught of the church this morning."

DRAUGHT. 61 lbs., or a quarter of a pack of wool (240 lbs.), with one pound allowed for the turn of the scale.

DRAW. A stratagem or device whereby a person is caught or drawn as it were into a trap.

DRAY, or DRAW. A squirrel's nest.
On St. Andrew's day, November 30, there was in former times an annual diversion called squirrel hunting, when crowds of people went out into the woods with sticks and guns, with which they not only destroyed squirrels, but anything that came in their way. This custom was kept up in Sussex till within the last fifty years, but now, in consequence of the inclosure of coppices and more strict preservation of game, it is wholly discontinued.

DREAN, *m.* A drain.

DREDGE. A mixture of oats and barley, now very little sown.

DREDGE, *m.* [*Drœge*, Ang. Sax., a drag.] A quantity of bushes, chiefly of thorn, bound together and drawn over meadows for the purpose of pulverizing dung or mould, called also a bush-harrow.

DRIB. [*Dripan*, Ang. Sax, to drop.] A very small quantity of anything.

DRIFTWAY, *m.* [*Drífan*, Ang. Sax., to drive.] A cattle-path to water; a way by which sheep or cattle are driven, generally a greenway from high ground to low.

DRINK, *m.* Medicine for cattle.
"I gave the old cow a drink last night, and she's up again and looking eversmuch better this morning."

DRINKER ACRE, *e.* The land set apart on dividing brook-land (which was depastured in common) for mowing, to provide drink and provisions for the tenants and labourers.

DRILLATY, *m.* [Corruption of Dilatory.]

DROPHANDKERCHIEF. The game of kiss-in-the ring.

DROVE-ROAD. An unenclosed road through a farm leading to different fields.

DRUGGED, *e.* Half dried; said of linen, &c.

DRUV. Driven. "I wunt be druv" is a favourite maxim with Sussex people.

DRYTHE. [*Drugath*, Ang. Sax.] Drought.
"Drythe never yet bred dëarth." —*Sussex Proverb*.

DUBBY, *e.* Short; blunt.
"I be dubersome whether she'll ever make a needlewoman, her fingers be so dubby."

DUBERSOME, *m.* Doubtful. This Anglo-Saxon form of termination is not uncommon in Sussex; we find it in timersome for timid, wearisome, and other words.

DUFF. This word, which is evidently only a variation of dough, is used for a pudding made with no other ingredients but flour and water; sometimes called hard dick.

DUFFER, *e.* A pedlar. This word is applied only to a hawker of women's clothes.

DUMBLEDORE, *w.* The humble bee.

DUNCH, *w.* Deaf; slow of comprehension.

DUNG-CART RAVES, *w.* A frame-work fitted on to a cart to accommodate an extra load.

DUNNAMANY, *m.* I do not know how many.
"There was a dunnamany people come to see that gurt hog of mine when she was took bad, and they all guv it in as she was took with the information. We did all as ever we could for her. There was a bottle of stuff what I had from the doctor, time my leg was so bad, and we took and mixed it in with some milk and give it her lew warm, but naun as we could give her didn't seem to do her any good."

DUNNAMUCH, *m.* I do not know how much.
"She cost me a dunnamuch for sharps and pollard and one thing and t'other."

DUP, *e.* To walk quickly.
"You was dupping along so, I knew you was late."

DUTCH COUSINS, *e.* Great friends. This expression is only used along the coast.
"Yes, he and I were reg'lar Dutch cousins; I feels quite lost without him."

DWAIRS, *w.* Strong cross-bars in the floor of a waggon. The one in the centre is called the fore-dwair, the one at the back, the hind-dwair. They are also called the cuts.

E.

EARSH, *w.* A stubble field; as a wheat earsh, a barley earsh—frequently pronounced ash.

EARTH. To turn up the ground as a mole does.

EDDEL. [Ang. Sax., *ádl*, corrupted.] Rotten.

EELSHEAR, *e.* An iron instrument with three or four points, fastened to the end of a long pole, by means of which it is thrust into muddy ponds and ditches for the purpose of catching eels.

E'EN-A'MOST. [Corruption of even almost.] Nearly.

"'Tis e'en-a'most time you gave over eelshearing for this year."

EFFET, *m.* [*Efete*, Ang. Sax.] A newt or eft. Dry efts are those found in the earth under hedge banks, and are said by the country people to be poisonous.

EGG. [*Eggian*, Ang. Sax., to excite.] To urge on; to incite.

ELDERN. Made of elder. (See Ether.)

ELEVENER, *w.* A luncheon. In Durham the haymakers and reapers call their afternoon meal in the field their "four o'clock."

ELLAR and ELLET, *e.* [*Elarn*, Ang. Sax.] The elder tree.

ELLER. The alder tree.

ELLEM and ELVEN, *m.* [*Ellm*, Sax.] The elm.

ELLYNGE, *m.* [*Ellende*, Ang. Sax., foreign.] Solitary; far from neighbours; uncanny.

"'Tis a terrible ellynge lonesome old house, and they do say as how there's a man walks under them gurt elven trees o'nights, but I've never seen him myself."

END-ON, *e.* In a great hurry.

"He went at it end on, as though he meant to finish afore he begun."

ENEW. Enough.

ERNFUL. Sad; lamentable.

ETHER, or EDDER. [Ang. Sax., *éther, édor*.] A hedge. A piece of pliant underwood, wound between the stakes of a new-made hedge.

> "An eldern stake and blackthorn ether
> Will make a hedge to last for ever."

EYED-AND-LIMBED, *m.* "He eyed and limbed me" means, he anathematized my eyes and limbs.

F.

FAD. A whim.

FADDY. Fanciful.

FAG, *w.* To cut corn or stubble close to the ground.

FAG-HOOK. A hook or bill fastened on a long stick for trimming hedges, or for fagging corn.

FAGOT, *m.* A good-for-nothing girl.

FAGOT-ABOVE-A-LOAD, *e.* Rather too much of a good thing.

> "Well, I do call it a fagot-above-a-load, to have to go down to Mr. Barham's twice a day."

FAIL. To fall ill; generally used of catching complaints.

> "He looks to me very much as though he was going to fail with the measles."

FAIRY-RINGS. Circles of grass which are higher, and of a deeper green than the grass which grows round them; attributed to the dancing of the fairies.

> "Ye elves—you demy-puppets, that by moonshine do the green sour ringlets make, whereof the ewe not bites."
> —*Tempest*, Act v. sc. 1.

FAIRY-SPARKS, *e.* Phosphoric light seen on various substances in the night-time.

FALL, *m.* The autumn.

> "I have the ague every spring and fall."

FALL. [*Feallan*, Ang. Sax.] To cut down timber.

> "These trees are getting too thick, I shall fall a few of them next year."

FAN, *e.* To banter; to tease.

> "Be not angry,
> Most mighty princess, that I have adventured
> To try your taking of a false report.
> *   *   The love I bear him
> Made me to fan you thus; but the Gods made you,
> Unlike all others, chaffless. Pray you pardon."
> —*Cymbeline*, Act i. sc. 7.

A Dictionary of the Sussex Dialect. 41

Fanner, *w*. A hawk.

Farisees. [*Fairieses.*] Fairies.

By an unfortunate use of the reduplicated plural, the Sussex country people confuse the ideas of fairies and Pharisees in a most hopeless manner. A belief in fairies is by no means extinct in the South Down districts, and among other stories the following was most seriously told me,—

"I've heard my feäther say, that when he lived over the hill, there was a carter that worked on the farm along wid him, and no one couldn't think how t'was that this here man's horses looked so much better than what any one else's did. I've heard my feäther say that they was that fat that they couldn't scarcely get about; and this here carter he was just as much puzzled as what the rest was, so cardinley he laid hisself up in the stäable one night, to see if he could find the meaning an't.

"And he hadn't been there very long, before these here liddle farisees they crep in at the sink hole; in they crep, one after another; liddle tiny bits of chaps they was, and each an 'em had a liddle sack of corn on his back as much as ever he could carry. Well! in they crep, on they gets, up they clims, and there they was, just as busy feeding these here horses; and prensley one says to t'other, he says, 'Puck,' says he, 'I twets, do you twet?' And thereupon, this here carter he jumps up and says, 'Dannel ye,' he says, 'I'll make ye twet afore I've done wud ye!' But afore he could get anigh 'em they was all gone, every one an 'em. "And I've heard my feäther say, that from that day forard this here carter's horses fell away, till they got that thin and poor that he couldn't bear to be seen along wid 'em, so he took and went away, for he couldn't abear to see hisself no longer; and nobody aint seen him since."

Fat-hen. The plant *chenopodium album*; called also goosefoot.

Favour, *m*. To resemble; a resemblance.

Duke Sen: "I do remember in this shepherd boy some lively touches of my daughter's favour.

Orla: "My Lord, the first time that I ever saw him methought he was a brother of your daughter."
—*As You Like It*, Act v. sc. 4.

Fay. To prosper; to go on favourably. " It fays well," sounds as if it was closely connected with *il fait bien*.

Fegs. An exclamation.

"Why! you are smart, fegs!"

Festical, *e*. [Corruption of Festival.] A feast.

"There ain't agoing to be any school festical to-year."

Fetch. A trick; a stratagem; a false appearance.
> "Mere fetches;
> The images of revolt and flying off."
> —*King Lear*, Act ii. sc. 4.

Fid. To work too hard at anything. In Yorkshire the word foy has the same meaning.

Fight. To flog. A standing complaint of parents against a school-teacher is "I wants more learning and less fighting."

File. A cunning, deceitful person.
In the same sense the word is used in speaking of a hare running her file.

Fill-dick, *m.* The month of February.
> "February fill the dick,
> Every day white or black."
> —*Sussex Proverb.*

Fire-fork, *w.* An iron prong for raking ashes out of the oven.

Fire-spannel, *m.* A lazy person, who is always sitting by the fireside.

Firm, *m.* A form; a bench without a back.

Fitches. Vetches.

Fitting, *m.* Proper; right.
"I didn't think it was at all fitting that he should call me over, and bellick about house same as he did, just because his supper wasn't ready dracly minute."

Fitty. Subject to fits.
The following extract from the Selmeston parochial account-book shows how afflicted persons were dealt with in former times,—
"Ladiday, 1790. This is an agreement which is between the Churchwardens and Overseers and Parishioners of the Parish of Selmeston, in the County of Sussex.
"The said parishioners do agree that R. Hillman should take Jas. Norman at two shillings and sixpence per week so long as he continues in the fitty state, but when Mr. Hillman shall give it in that he can work well, and equal with other boys, he, the said Hillman, will do and keep him, the said boy, for as little and little money as any parishioner shall think proper."

Flake, *e.* Cleft wood.

Flam, *w.* A small net used in ferreting to cover the rabbit-holes.

Flap, *w.* A large broad mushroom.

A Dictionary of the Sussex Dialect.

FLAPPERS, *e.* Pieces of wood which the fishermen strap over their boots when they walk on the shingle. (See Backsters.)

FLAPPERS. Young wild ducks which have just taken to the wing but are unable to fly.

FLAP JACK. A sort of tart made of apples baked without a pan, in a thin piece of paste; also called apple turnover.

FLASKET, *w.* [*Fflasget*, Welsh, a shallow basket.] A clothes basket; a shallow washing tub.

FLAT, *m.* A hollow in a field.
"The water lays so in these flats."

FLAW, *m.* To strip bark; to flay.
"He's got a job of tan-flawing."

FLECK, *m.* FLICK, or FLOX. [*Flys*, Ang. Sax., fleece; down.] The fur of hares or rabbits.
"A pillowbedde stuffed with fflox." —*Inventory*, 1549.
"Old Mus Crackshott left two robbuts down at our house when he come to fetch his rent o' Saddaday. Purty much knocked about they was—so my mistus she put 'em into a pudden for Sunday, but when we come to set down to dinner they'd biled theirselves all away, and all the robbut as we could find was fower ounces of duck shot and some liddle bits of fleck for flavouring! and I says to my mistus, I says, 'If these be Mus Crackshott's robbuts I'd as lief have bren-cheese.'"

FLEED. [*Flèche*, French.] The inside fat of a hog before it is melted into lard.

FLEED-CAKES. Cakes made with fresh fleed: an indispensable adjunct to the family festival of pig-killing.

FLEET, *e.* To be set afloat.
A vessel is said to fleet when the tide flows sufficiently to enable her to move.

FLIGHT. To go to flight is to shoot wild ducks or plover at twilight.
"There was three of our chaps went out t'otherday evening purty nigh up as fur as Laughton to flight; but all as ever they brought home along wid 'em was Master Pelts, the shoemaker, as had gone up on the quiet two hours afore, and laid hisself up along wid a gurt bottle of whiskey; and when they got up to the brooks there he was a layin' on his back and a hollerin' of hisself hoarse, and shootin' up in the air at the rooks a-going over to Furrel, till they was forced to take his gun away from him and carry him home."

Flindermouse, *e;* **Flittermouse**, *m;* or **Fluttermouse**, *w.* A bat.

Flit, *m.* Shallow; thin.
When water is low it is said to be flit; and land is flit when there is only a slight layer of good earth upon it.

Flit, *e.* [*Flet*, Ang. Sax., cream.] A milk skimmer.

Flit, *e.* A bat. A bat coming indoors is considered an evil omen.

Flit-milk. Skim milk.

Flog, *m.* To tire; to be wearied out.
"I was fairly flogged by the time I got home."

Flounders. Animals found in the livers of rotten sheep; also called flooks.

Floush-hole. [*Fluissen*, Dutch, to flow fast.] A hole which receives the waste water from a mill pond.

Flower. [Corruption of Floor.]

Flown-in, *e.* To be overtaken by the tide.
"You're too oudacious daring on they sands; if you doänt mind you'll be flown in, one of these days."

Flue. [*Flaauw*, Dutch, weak; feeble.] Delicate; a flue horse is one which always looks thin, and will not carry flesh.

Flushy, *e.* Swampy; as ground after a continuance of wet weather.

Fluttergrub, *m.* A man who takes a delight in working about in the dirt, and getting into every possible mess.

Flux, *e.* To snatch at anything; to blush.

Fly Golding, *e.* The ladybird. (See Bishop Barnaby.)

Fob, *e.* To froth as beer does.

Fob, *e.* The froth of beer; the foam on a horse's mouth.

Fog, *w.* Long grass growing in pastures in late summer or autumn, not fed down, but allowed to stand through the winter.

Folding-bar, *w.* An iron bar used for making the holes in which the wattles are fixed for folding the sheep.

Fold-tare, or **Fold-tail**, *m.* The improvement of land caused by sheep having been folded on it.

Footy. Silly; foolish; worthless.

A Dictionary of the Sussex Dialect.

Forced. Obliged.

"I was forced to putt on my spartacles."

Fordrough, *e.* A cattle-path to water; a grass ride.

Fore, *m.* Front. In Yorkshire the spring is called "the fore-end of the year."

Fore-door, *m.* The front door.

Fore-horse, *m.* "He has got the fore-horse by the head" is a Sussex expression for "he has got matters well in hand."

Forecast, *m.* Forethought.

Foreigner. A stranger; a person who comes from any other county but Sussex.

At Rye, in East Sussex, that part of the parish which lies out of the boundary of the corporation, is called the Foreign of Rye.

I have often heard it said of a woman in this village, who comes from Lincolnshire, that "she has got such a good notion of work that you'd never find out but what she was an Englishwoman, without you was to hear her talk."

Foreright. Plain spoken; rude; obstinate.

"I doänt know whatever I shall do with that boy, he's so foreright, and he doänt seem to have no forecast of nothing."

Fore-summer, *w.* The top rail in front of a waggon. The corresponding rail at the back is called the hawk.

Forstall, or **Fostel,** *m.* [Ang. Sax., *fore*, before; and *steal*, a stall, place, or stead.] The house and home buildings of a farm with waste land attached.

Fornicate, *m.* To dawdle; to waste time.

Forrep-land, *w.* Used in the manor of Bosham for assart land, or land from which the wood or forest has been cut down, to bring it into cultivation.

Fother. To feed cattle.

Foundle, *m.* Anything found.

"I picked up a foundle yesterday, as I was coming home off the hill."

Fourthrows, or **Fourwents,** *e.* A place where four roads meet. (See Went.)

Frail, *m.* Flail.

> "Dame Durden kept five serving men
> To use the spade and frail."

Frayel, *m.* A flexible basket made of bulrushes, commonly used for packing game.

Frenchy, *e.* A foreigner of any country who cannot speak English, the nationality being added or not, as the case seems to require; thus an old fisherman, giving an account of a Swedish vessel which was wrecked on the coast a year or two ago, finished by saying that he thought the French Frenchys, take 'em all in all, were better than the Swedish Frenchys, for he could make out what they were driving at, but he was all at sea with the others.

Fresh, *m.* Home-brewed small beer, which must be drunk while new or fresh.

Fresh, *e.* To decorate; to renew.
"I freshed up my bonnet with those ribbons you gave me."

Fresh, *e.* Fresh air.
"It feels very close to you coming in out of the fresh, but Jane she's had her fevers all day, and I dursn't set the the window open to let in any fresh, for I was afraid 'twould give her cold."

Fresh. Not quite drunk, but rather noisy.

Frit, *e.* Frightened.
"I was quite frit to see him so near the water."

Frith, *e.* Young underwood; brushwood growing by the side of hedges.

Frore, *w.* Frozen. Spenser uses frorne in the same sense.

Frostbeck, *w.* A strong handbill for cutting up turnips when they are frozen.

Frouden, *m;* or **Frought,** *w.* Frightened.

I met an elderly man one evening going through the churchyard; it was too dark to see who he was, and I passed without speaking. To my surprise he stopped and began shouting as loud as he could; and recognising his voice, I went back to ask him what was the matter. "Oh dear me, sir!" he said, "is that you? I didn't know it was you, sir, I'm sure I beg your pardon." It was in vain that I enquired why he was making such a dreadful noise; no answer could I get, beyond that he didn't know who it was. So I wished him good night and went on, under the impression that he was drunk; but the matter was explained by his turning back to say, "I beg your pardon, sir, but I hope you doänt think I was frouden! Bless me, no! I was noways frouden, not at all! I'm a man as aint easily frouden at meeting anyone in the churchyard after dark."

FURLONG. A division of tenantry land.

FURNAGE, *w*. A sum formerly paid by the tenants of the lord of the manor for right to bake in his oven.

FUTTICE, *e*. A weazel.

G.

GABERDINE, *m*. A loose frock still worn in Sussex by farm labourers.
> "My best way is to creep under his gaberdine."
> —*Tempest*, Act ii. sc. 2.

GAFFER, *m*. Abbreviation of grandfather.

GAFFER, *m*. A master.
"Gaffer has given me a holiday."

GAGY, *e*. Showery.

GALLEYBIRD, or GALLOWSBIRD. The woodpecker.

GALORE.* In abundance. This old Celtic word is still in common use in Scotland and Ireland.

GALLOWS. To die under the gallows is said to be the fate of a person who dies of overwork.

GAMELING, *e*. [*Gamen*, Ang. Sax., a game.] Romping about.

GAMMER, *m*. Abbreviation of grandmother.

GANSE, *e*. Merriment; hilarity.

GANSING-GAY, *e*. Cheerful; lively.
> "Some people said the children would always be interrupting of us if we went to live so near the school, but for my part I likes to hear them, their voices is so gansing gay its quite company to me."

GAP, *m*. [*Geapu*, Ang. Sax., a space.] An opening through the chalk cliffs on the Southdowns leading to the sea, as Birling Gap, Copperas Gap, &c.; also called a gut.

GAPE SEED.* Something to stare at. A person staring out of window is said to be sowing gape seed.

GARATWIST.* Altogether on one side.

Garreting, *w.* Small pieces of flint stuck in the mortar courses in building.

Gaskin, *e.* [Gascony.] A kind of cherry largely grown in the neighbourhood of Rye, which is called indifferently "geen" or "gaskin," having been brought from France by Joan of Kent when her husband, the Black Prince, was commanding in Guienne and Gascony.

In olden days a Lord of Berkeley finding housekeeping too costly, agreed with the widow of a Kentish nobleman for lodging and maintenance of himself, his wife, her two waiting women, six serving men, and horses for the whole party at £200 a year, but he died before the year was out of eating too many gaskins.

Gate, *w.* A farmyard.

Gaunt, *e.* [*Geanian,* Ang. Sax.] To yawn.

Gay-ground, *e.* A flower garden.

"I likes to have a bit of gayground under the window for a look out."

Gazels, *e.* [*Groseiller,* a currant tree.] All kinds of berries, but especially black currants.

Gazel tea is a favourite remedy for a cold.

Geat. [*Geat,* Ang. Sax., a gate.] The Anglo-Saxon form of the word is always used for gate in Sussex.

Gee, *m.* To get on well with a person.

"We've lived up agin one another for a good many years, and we've always geed together very nicely."

Geemeny, *m.* [Corruption of O Gemini!]

"Geemeny! you do mean to be spicy."

Geen, *e.* [*Guienne,* French.] (See Gaskin.)

Gee-woot. An expression used by waggoners to make the leading horse go to the off side; to the shaft horse the word for the same purpose is hoot.

Generally-always, *m.* A superlative form of generally.

"My master generally-always comes home none the better for what he's had of a Saddaday night."

Gentleman, *m.* A person who does not earn his own living. Anyone who is disabled from work. The term is sometimes applied to a sick woman, or even to a horse.

"I'm sure I've done all I could for mother; if she isn't a gentleman I should like to know who is!"

GIFTS. White specks which appear on the finger nails, supposed to indicate the arrival of a present.
> "A gift on the thumb, is sure to come;
> A gift on the finger is sure to linger."

GIFTY, *w.* [*Giftig*, Dutch.] Unwholesome; poisonous.
> "The house smelt quite gifty-like."

GIGGLESOME. Given to giggle.

GIMSY, *e.* Smartly dressed.

GIVE-IN. To state an opinion.
> "Master Cockleshaw he gives it in that we shall have a change of weather before many days."

GIVE-OVER. Leave off.
> "You just give over messing-about among my cabbages."

GLINCY. [*Glincer*, Old French, to slide.] Smooth; slippery; applied to ice.

GLUM. [*Glôm*, Ang. Sax., gloom.] Gloomy.
> "The weather looks very glum this morning."

GNANG, *e.* [*Gnagan*, Ang. Sax., to gnaw.] To gnash the teeth.

GOAD, *w.* Any long stick. Pronounced góad.

GOBBET. [*Gobet*, French, a hasty meal.] A large mouthful of anything; a lump.
> "Meet I an infant of the house of York,
> Into as many gobbets will I cut it,
> As wild Medea young Absyrtus did."
> —II *Henry VI.*, Act v. sc. 2.

GOLD CUP. The meadow ranunculus.

GOLE. [*Gole*, Old French, the gullet.] A wooden drain pipe. In the north of England the word is used for a small stream.

GOODEN, or GOODENING. The custom of going from house to house for doles on St. Thomas's day (21st December). This was done by women only, and a widow had a right to a double dole; the presumed object being to obtain money or provisions for the enjoyment of the approaching festival of Christmas.

GOODMAN. An old title of address to the master of the house.
I find the following entries in a book of accounts of the parish of Selmeston,—

1745, December ye 22.

"Goodman Gasson

payd fower men for Carring John Gasson to the ground	00 .. 04 .. 00
payd Tho. Jurden for buring John Gasson	00 .. 02 .. 06
payd for laying John Gasson foarth and one shilling for ather Daved" (affidavit)	00 .. 03 .. 00

Goody. The title of an elderly widow.

> Expences for the yeare 1743:
> Payd Goody Gorge for washing and mending her suns
> cloath and Goody Pumphery 6 pence . . . . . . 01 .. 00 .. 06

Gossip, *e.* [*Gobsibb,* Ang. Sax., a sponsor.] This word is still used, though very rarely, by old people.

> "They've brought a child to be christened, but they haven't got no gossips."

Go-under. Undergo.

> "The doctor says he must go to the hospital and go under an operation."

Grabby, *e.* Grimy; filthy; dirty.

Graff, or **Graffing-tool,** *m.* [*Grafan,* Ang. Sax., to dig.] A curved spade, generally made of wood shod with iron, used by drainers.

Grandfather, *m.* A daddy-long-legs.

Gratten, *m.* A stubble field.

Gratten. [*Gratter,* French, to scratch.] To scratch for the grain that may be left on the grattens.

> "By the time the pigs have been grattening for a week they'll look eversmuch better."

Grew, *e.* A greyhound.

Greybeards, *m.* Earthen jugs formerly used in public-houses for beer, and so called from having on them the face of a man with a large beard.

Greybird, *m.* The thrush.

Grib, *e.* Variation of grip. A sharp bite.

Gridgen, *m.* Grudging; stingy.

> "If he has anything given him, he's that gridgen that he'll never give away naun an't."

Grig, *e.* Merry; happy.

> "Master Harry he's always so grig."

Grip. [*Groep,* Ang. Sax.] A small ditch or drain.

Grizzle, *m.* To fret; to grieve.

> "I know the child aint well, because she's been grizzling about so all day, and she's never one to grizzle when she's well."

Grom, *e.* [*Grommeler,* Dutch, to wallow.] Dirty; to soil or make dirty.

GROOM, *m.* An instrument used by thatchers for carrying bundles of straw.

GROUT-HEADED. Stupidly noisy.

GRUBBY, *e.* To make in a mess.

"You've grubbied your pinney," means "you have dirtied your pinafore."

GRUMMUT. An awkward boy.

Mr. M. A. Lower states that this word is a corruption of the old French, *gromet*, a diminutive of groom; the cabin-boy of the Cinque Ports navy was so called. The condition of the distinguished immunities of those ancient corporations was, that they should provide for the King's use a certain number of ships, and in each ship twenty-one men, with one boy, called a gromet—"*et in qualibit nave xxi. homines, cum uno garcione qui dicitur gromet.*"

—*Suss. Arch. Coll.* vol. xiii. p. 217.

GRYST. [*Grist*, Ang. Sax., a grinding.] A week's allowance of flour for a family.

GUBBER, *e.* Black mud.

GUDGE, *m.* To probe.

"The doctor came and vaccinated our baby yesterday; nasty man! he just did gudge his poor little arm about."

GUESS-SHEEP, *m.* Young ewes that have been with the ram and had no lambs; so called because it is doubtful or a matter of guess whether they will ever have lambs.

GULL, *w.* To sweep away by force of running water; a breach made by a torrent.

GULL. A gosling.

GULL, *m.* The blossom of the willow; called in Cambridgeshire goslins.

GUMMUT. A lout; a stupid fellow. (See Grummut.)

GUMPTIOUS, *e.* Smart; tawdry.

GUN, *m.* To examine carefully; to con over.

"When I gunned her over a little closer, I soon saw that she was too gumptious by half to be a lady."

GURGISE, *w.* A fish-pool; lake, or pond.

GURT. [Corruption of Great.]

GUT, *m.* [*Gjota*, Icel.; *Gota*, Ang. Sax., a pourer.] An underground drain for water.

GUTTERDICK, *m.* A small drain.

"'Taint no use at all for you to make that 'ere gutterdick, what you wants is a gurt gut."

GYLE. A brewing of beer.

H.

HABERN, *w.* The back of the grate.

"Why, whatever have you been a-doing with yourself? Your face is as black as a habern!"

HACK. To cough faintly and frequently.

HACK, *w.* To rake up hay into thin rows.

HACKER, *m.* To stutter and stammer.

HACK-HOOK, *m.* [*Haccan,* Ang. Sax., to cut.] A curved hook with a long handle, used for cutting peas and tares, or trimming hedges.

HACKLE, *m.* [*Hœcele,* Ang. Sax., a garment.] A straw covering placed over beehives.

HAFFER, or HARFER. A heifer.

"I leave to Jane, my wife's daughter, an haffer of 2 yerys age." —*Will of Thos. Donet, of Burwash,* 1542.

HAGRIDDEN, *m.* To be hagridden is to have the nightmare.

HAGTRACK, *m.* Circles of coarse green grass seen on the meadows and downs, supposed to be tracks of hags or witches who have danced there at night.

HAITCH, *e.* A slight passing shower.

HAITCHY, *e.* Misty.

HALF-BAPTIZED. Privately baptized.

"If you please, Sir, will you be so good as to half-baptize the baby?" "Oh! certainly; but which half of him am I to baptize?"

HALF-BAPTIZED, *e.* Silly, foolish.

"You must have been half-baptized to water those flowers when the sun was full on them."

HALF-HAMMER, *w.* The game of hop-step-and-jump.

HALF-SWING PLOUGH, *w.* A plough in which the mould-board is a fixture.

HAM. [Ang. Sax., *hám;* German, *heim;* English, *home.*] A level pasture field; a plot of ground near a river.

"In the country of the Angles as well as here (in North Friesland) every enclosed place is called a hamm."
—*Outzen's Glossary of the Frisian Language,* p. 113.

HAMPERY, *m.* [Possibly from *empiré*, French, decayed.] Out of repair.

HAMWOOD, *w.* [*Hame-wood.*] Pieces of wood on the collar of a horse to which the traces are fixed.

HAND, *m.* To be a hand, is to cause a great deal of trouble.
"I was a terrible hand to mother all the time I was down with the titus-fever."

HANDLE-DISH, *m.* A bowl with a handle.

HANGER, *m.* A hanging wood on a hill side.

HANSEL, *m;* or HACKLE, *e.* To use anything for the first time.

HANSEL, *m.* [*Handsylen*, Ang. Sax., a giving into the hands.] The first money received in the morning for the sale of goods. The market women have a custom of kissing the first coin, spitting on it, and putting it in a pocket by itself for luck.

HAP, *m.* Perhaps.

HAPPEN-ALONG, *m.* To come by chance; to arrive unexpectedly.
"Master Tumptops, he's a man as you'll notice mostly happens-along about anyone's dinner-time."

HAPS, *m.* [*Hæps*, Ang. Sax.] Hasp of a door or box.

HARD-DICK. Sussex pudding, made of flour and water only.

HARNESS, *m.* Temper; humour.
"Master's in purty good harness this morning."

HAROLD. A common Christian name in East Sussex, which is always pronounced the same as the word earl.

HASSOCK, *e.* [Possibly from *Haso*, Ang. Sax., dry; rugged.] Anything growing in a thick matted state. A thick wooded shaw or little wood.

HATCH, *m.* To sicken for any complaint.
"I think she's hatching the measles." This expression seems to correspond very closely with that used by physicians when they speak of the period of incubation.

HATCH, *m.* To dress the bark of trees.

HATCH. In names of places probably means a gate.
It is usually found on the borders of forests, as Coleman's Hatch, Plaw-hatch and Claw-hatch, in Ashdown forest.

HATCH, *w.* A gate; a half-door.

HATCHEL, *w.* To rake cut grass into small rows.

HAULM. [*Healm*, Ang. Sax.] The straw of beans, peas, tares, &c.

HAUST, *m.* A place for drying hops. (See Oast-house.)

HAVE, *m.* To lead or take.
"I shall have him down to his grandmother while I go haying."

HAVILER, or HEAVER, *e.* [*Heafer*, Ang. Sax.] A crab.

HAWK, *w.* (See Fore-summer.)

HAYWARD, *w.* [Haw-ward; hedge-ward.] An officer of the lord of the manor, whose business it was to look after the hedges and see that the boundaries were kept right.

HEAD, *m.* "To your head" is the same as "to your face."
"I told him to his head that I wouldn't have such goings-on in my house any more."
"To the head of Angelo accuse him home and home."
—*Measure for Measure*, Act iv. sc. 2.

HEAD-ACHE, *e.* The corn poppy. *Papaver rhœas.*

HEADLANDS, *m.* The part of the field close against the hedges.

HEADPIECE, *m.* The head considered with regard to the intellect.
"He's got a very good headpiece, and if he could have had a little more schooling he'd have made something better than a ploughboy."

HEAL, *m.* [*Hêlan*, Ang. Sax., to cover or conceal.] To cover.
"I healed up the roots with some straw."
"In the ancient English dialect the word 'hell' was taken in a large sense for the general receptacle of all souls whatsoever, and it is so used in the old translation of the Psalms in our Common Prayer Book (Ps. lxxxix. 47), which sense may be confirmed from the primary and original signification of the word; according to which it imports no more than an invisible and hidden place, being derived from the old Saxon word '*hil*,' which signifies to hide, or from the participle thereof, *helled*, that is to say, hidden or covered; as in the western parts of England, at this very day, to '*hele*' over any-

A Dictionary of the Sussex Dialect.

thing, signifies, amongst the common people, to cover it, and he that covereth an house with tile or slate is called an '*hellier;*' whence it appears that the word '*hell*,' according to its primitive notion, exactly answers to the Greek '*hades*' which signifies the common mansion of departed souls, and was so called because it is an unseen place."

—*Lord Chancellor King on the Apostle's Creed*, pp. 233, 193, 194 Ed. Lond. 1702.

HEALED. [*Hyldan*, Ang. Sax., to incline.] When a ship goes over to one side she is said to have healed over.

HEALING, *m.* A coverlet; a counterpane.

In the will of Rev. H. Marshall, he leaves "2 pillowberes and a healing."

HEART, *m.* Condition; said of ground.

"I've got my garden into pretty good heart at last, and if so be as there warnt quite so many sparrs and greybirds and roberts and one thing and t'other, I dunno but what I might get a tidy lot of sass. But there! taint no use what ye do as long as there's so much varmint about."

HEAVE-GATE, *m.* [*Hefan* and *geat*, Ang. Sax.] A low gate, so constructed as to lift out from the posts, instead of opening with hinges.

HEDGE-HOG. Venus' comb. *Scandix pecten-veneris.*

HEDGE-PICK, or HEDGE-MIKE, *m.* The hedge sparrow.

HEEN, *m.* [*Hæn*, Ang. Sax.] A hen.

"I throwed a stone at a liddle hedge-pick a settin' on the heave-geat, and killed Mrs. Pankurstes' gurt old packled heen."

HEGGLING. Vexatious; trying; wearisome.

HEIRS.* Young timber trees.

HELP, *m.* To give anything into a person's hands.

"I will help the letter to him if you'll write a few lines."

HELVE, *e.* To gossip.

HELVE, *e.* A long gossip.

HEM, *m.* Very.

"Hem crusty old chap our shepherd is, surelye! I says to him yesterday, I says, ' 'Tis hem bad weather, shepherd,' I says. 'Ah,' says he, ' 'tis better than no weather at all;' and hem-a-bit would he say any more."

HEM-A-BIT, *m.* Not a bit; certainly not.

HEMMEL, *e.* A fold. Connected with the Icelandic word *hemja*, to restrain.

HENRIP, *w.* A hen-coop.

HERE-AND-THERE-ONE. An expression used to signify an average, or on an average, as "He aint much of a boy I know, but he's quite as good a boy as you'll find here-and-there-one."

HIDE. [*Hyd*, Ang. Sax.] A hide of land is about 120 acres. In Saxon times it meant as much land as could be tilled with one plough; a family possession.

HIGGLER, *m.* A huckster; so called from higgling over his bargains.

HIKE, *m.* To call roughly.
"He hiked me out of the pew."

HILL, *m.* The Southdown country is always spoken of as "The hill" by the people in the Weald.
"He's gone to the hill, harvesting."

HILL-UP, *m.* [*Hélan*, Ang. Sax., to cover.] To hill-up hops is to raise small hills or heaps over the roots for the purpose of keeping them dry in the winter.

HISN, *m.* His own.
The possessive pronoun is thus conjugated in Sussex,—
Mine, thine, hisn or hern.
Ourn, yourn, theirn.

HITHER, *m.* Near.
"He's in the hither croft."

HOBBLE, *m.* A doubt; an uncertainty.

HOB-LAMB, *m.* A pet lamb, brought up by hand.

HOB-UP. To bring up anything by hand.
A parishioner of mine once came to complain to me that her husband had threatened to ill-use her on account of two little pigs which she was hobbing-up; but as I found that his objection rested on the fact that she was hobbing-up the pigs so carefully that she insisted on taking them to bed with her, I declined to interfere.

HOCKLANDS. [*Hôh*, Ang. Sax., a heel.] Hock-shaped pieces of meadow land. —*Leo's Ang. Sax. Names.*

HOCK-MONDAY, *w.* The second Monday after Easter, kept as a festival in remembrance of the defeat of the Danes in King Ethelred's time.

HOE, *w.* Fuss; anxiety.

"I doänt see as you've any call to putt yourself in no such terrible gurt hoe over it."

HOGARVES, *m.* Hog-gazels; hawthorn berries.

HOG-FORM, *w.* A bench on which pigs are laid to be killed and dressed.

On the knuckle of a pig's fore-leg there are always six marks, about the size of a pea, which are believed to have been caused by the devil's fingers when he entered the herd of swine.

HOGGET, *w.* A young sheep, just more than a year old.

HOG-JET, *w.* A small bucket, fastened into a long handle, by which the food is taken out of the hog-tub.

HOGO.* [*Haut gout*, French.] A strong foul smell.

HOGPOUND, *m.* The pigstye; a favourite rendezvous on Sundays.

"Ah! many's the time as we've stood over the hog-pound together, and looked 'em over, and rackoned 'em up, whiles people was in church; little did he think as he'd be putt in before that hog was killed! and he always allowed she'd weigh sixty stun."

HOLL, *e.* To hurl; to throw.

HOLLARDS.* Dead branches of trees.

HOLP, *m.* [*Healp*, Ang. Sax.] The perfect of help.

"She had me round to the pound, to see a little hogget what she'd hobbed-up; and then she had me indoors and holp me to a cup of tea and some honey-bread."

HOLT, *m.* [*Holt*, Ang. Sax., a grove.] A small plantation.

HOLT. A hold.

"'Tis just like a lawyer, if once it takes a holt 'an ye, ye doänt very easy get free agin."

HOLT, *m.* [Corruption of Halt.] A call always used to stop a person.

HOLY-SUNDAY, *e.* Easter-day.

There is a tradition that the sun always dances on the morning of Holy-Sunday, but nobody has even seen it because the devil is so cunning that he always puts a hill in the way to hide it.

HOME-DWELLERS, *m.* People accustomed to live in houses, as opposed to tramps.

"A good many of these people who've come harvesting this year, look like home-dwellers."

HONEY-BREAD. Bread and honey.

HOOKE, or HOOK. [*Hóc*, Ang. Sax., a hook.] A name given to several places in Sussex.

HOP-DOG, *m.* A caterpillar peculiar to the hop gardens.

HOP-DOG, *m.* An instrument used to draw the hop-poles out of the ground, for the purpose of carrying them to the bin to be picked.

HOP-HORSE, *e.* A short ladder used by the hop-pickers.

HOP-MAND, *w.* [*Mond*, Ang. Sax., a basket.] A vessel used in brew-houses.

HORN-FAIR, *m.* Rough music with frying pans, horns, &c., generally reserved for persons whose matrimonial difficulties have attracted the attention of their neighbours. The fair annually held in Charlton, Kent (now abolished), was always known as Horn fair.

HORNICLE, *w.* A hornet.

HORSEBEACH, or HUSBEECH, *w.* The hornbeam.

HORSE-DAISY, *w.* The ox-eye daisy. *Chrysanthemum leucanthemum*.

HOSTE, *e.* Described by Durrant Cooper as "A vendor of articles out of shops or houses," so used at Hastings. From the old French word Hoste, which meant both a host and a guest.

This word is used in the second sense,—a guest, a person allowed to come, a stranger.

"Every person not lotting or shotting to the common charge of the Corporation, who should be a common *hoste* in the fishmarket." —*Hastings Corporation Records*, 1604.

HOT, *m.* To warm up.

"I was that cold when I got indoors that gaffer hotted up some beer for me."

HOTAGOE. To move nimbly; spoken of the tongue.

HOT-CHILLS, *m.* The fever that accompanies the ague.

HOTH, *m.* Hawth. The name of Hoathly seems connected with this word.

"'Tis very poor ground, it wont grow naun but heath and hoth."

HOT-POT, *m.* Hot ale and spirits.

HOUNDS, *w.* The part of a wagon to which the fore-wheels and shafts are attached.

HOUSED, *e.* When hops have a great deal of bine, and the poles are thickly covered over the top, so as almost to shut out the light and sun, they are said to be "housed."

HOUSEL, *m.* Household goods.
"Whose housel is that up on the wagon?"

HOVELER, *e.* A pilot.

HOVELERS, *e.* Men who go out to sea in boats for the purpose of meeting homeward-bound vessels, and engaging with the captain to unload them when they enter the harbour.

HOVER, *m.* Light; spoken of the ground or soil.

HOVER, *m.* Looking cold and shivery.
"Some of the children looked middlin' hover as they went along to school this morning through the snow."

HOVER, *m.* To hover hops is to measure them lightly into the basket.

HOWK, *e.* To dig. Possibly connected with the Dutch word houwen, to hew.

HOWLERS, *w.* Boys who in former times went round wassailing the orchards. A custom now nearly obsolete.

The custom of wassailing used to be observed on the eve of the Epiphany, when the howlers went to the orchards, and there encircling one of the best bearing trees, drank the following toast,—

> "Here's to thee, old apple tree,
> May'st thou bud, may'st thou blow,
> May'st thou bear apples enow!
> Hats full! Caps full!
> Bushel, bushel, sacks full!
> And my pockets full, too! Huzza!"

The wassailers derived their name from the Anglo-Saxon salutation on pledging one to drink, which was *wæs hæl*, be of health; to which the person pledged replied *drinc hæl*, I drink your health.

HOWSUMDEVER, *m.* However.

HOX, *w.* To cut the hamstrings; to cut the sinew of a rabbit's leg and put the other foot through, in order to hang it up.

Huck, *e.* The pod of a pea.

> Children get the pods and cry to each other,—
> "Pea-pod hucks,
> Twenty for a pin;
> If you döant like 'em
> I'll take 'em back agin."

Huck, *e.* A hard blow or knock rudely given.

Huck, *e.* To spread anything about, such as manure.

Huckle-bone, *e.* The small bone found in the joint of the knee of a sheep, used by children for playing the game of dibs.

Dr. Clarke, in his travels in Russia, 1810, vol. I., p. 177, says,"In all the villages and towns from Moscow to Woronetz, as in other parts of Russia, are seen boys, girls, and sometimes old men, playing with the joint bones of sheep. This game is called dibbs by the English. It is of very remote antiquity; for I have seen it very beautifully represented on Grecian vases, particularly on a vase in the collection of the late Sir William Hamilton, where a female figure appeared most gracefully delineated kneeling upon one knee, with her right arm extended, the palm downwards, and the bones ranged along the back of her hand and arm; a second is in the act of throwing up the bones in order to catch them. In this manner the Russians play the game."

Huckle-my-buff, *e.* A beverage composed of beer, eggs and brandy.

Huckmuck, *w.* A wicker strainer used in brewing.

Huff, *e.* To scold or take to task.

Huffy, *e.* Liable to take offence.

Hugger-mugger, *m.* In disorder; without system.

> "We have done but greenly in hugger-mugger to inter him."
> —*Hamlet*, Act iv. sc. 5.

Hull, *e.* To throw. (See Holl.)

Hull, *m.* [*Hulze*, Dutch, a shell of a pea; a case.] The husk or chaff of corn; the shell of a nut; the pod of peas.

Hull, *w.* To shell peas; to strip off the outside covering of anything.

Humble-cow, *e.* A cow without horns.

Hunch, *m.* A nudge.

> "I thought they were sweethearts, because I see him give her a hunch in church with his elbow."

Hung-up, *m.* Hindered.
"I was so hung up for time all last week I couldn't come."

Hurley-bulloo, *m.* A disturbance.

Hurr, *m.* Tart; rough-tasting.
"The doctor's ordered me to drink some of this here claret wine, but I shall never get to like it, it seems so hurr."

Hurst, *m.* [*Hurst*, Ang. Sax.] A wood.

Hurts, *w.* Whortle berries.

Huss, *m.* To hiss; to buzz; said of insects.
"The old owl I fancy did huss and spet when I went to take the eggs! and just did scratch a gurt pläàce in my harnd wud he's old to-a-nails, too."

Huss, *e.* To caress.
The children play a game, which is accompanied by a song beginning,—
"Hussing and bussing will not do,
But go to the gate, knock and ring,—
Please, Mrs. Brown, is Nellie within?"

Husser-and-Squencher, *e.* A pot of beer with a dram of gin in it. (See Squench.)

Hypocrite, *e.* A lame person.
This word may be possibly connected with, or a corruption of the old word *hippand*, meaning limping or hopping.
"Yes, she's a poor afflicted creature; she's quite a hypocrite; she can't walk a step without her stilts."

I.

Ice-Bone. The edge-bone of beef.

Ichon'em. Each one of them.

Idget, *w.* A horse hoe; called also a nidget or edget.

Ill-conditioned, *m.* Ill-tempered.
"He's the most ill-conditioned impersome young chap I know; a proper out-and-outener."

Ill-convenient, *m.* Inconvenient.

Impersome, *e.* Impertinent.

In, *w.* [*Innian*, Ang. Sax., to take in.] To inclose land.

"I inned that piece of land from the common."

An Anglo-Saxon estate was usually divided into two parts; one of which, called the *inland*, was occupied by the proprietor with his establishment; and the other, called the *utland*, was ceded to the servants in return for rent and service, as a reward for their assistance, or as the means of support to those who were not freed-men.

In, *w.* To house corn.

"The corn was all inned before Michaelmas-day."

Ing. [*Ing*, Ang. Sax.] A common pasture or meadow.

Ingenurious, *e.* Ingenious.

"For my part I consider that King Solomon was a very ingenurious man."

Ink-horn, *m.* Inkstand.

"Fetch me down de inkhorn, mistus; I be g'wine to putt my harnd to dis here partition to Parliament. 'Tis agin de Romans, mistus; for if so be as de Romans gets de upper harnd an us, we shall be burnded, and bloodshedded, and have our Bibles took away from us, and dere'll be a hem set out."

Innardly, *m.* Inaudibly; inwardly.

"This new parson of ours says his words so innardly."

Innocent, *m.* Small and pretty. Generally applied to flowers.

Innings, *w.* Land that has been enclosed from the sea. (See In.)

Interrupt, *m.* To attack.

This word is used to express all kinds and degrees of assault.

Item.* A hint.

Inward, *m.* Silent; reserved.

"I can't abear going to work along ud Master Meopham, he be so inward."

Inwards. Intestines.

A story is told in the neighbourhood of Rye of an old man who informed the clergyman after he had been preaching about veracity, that he thought his a capital good sermon, but he did not know what he meant by saying so much about the innards of a hog.

Ix. [*Ex*, Ang. Sax., an axis.] An axle tree.

J.

Jack-hearn, *m.* A heron; always spoken of as "a gurt old jack-hëarn."
"Parham Park, in West Sussex, can still boast of one of the most interesting heronries in the south of England."
—*Knox's Ornithological Rambles in Sussex.*

Jack-in-the-hedge, *e.* Lychnis diurna.

Jack-in-prison, *e.* Nigella damascena.

Jack-up, *m.* To give up anything in a bad temper.
A man came to my house by himself one Christmas Eve to sing carols, and at the end of each line he stopped to explain why the other singers were absent. He began,—
"While Shepherds watched their flocks by night."
"If you please, sir, my party's all jacked up"—
"All seated on the ground"—
"Yes, sir, there was young Harry down here, and my brother Jem, and Tom and George, we've all been a practising together, and now they're properly jacked up" (and so on to the end of the hymn).

Jacket, *m.* To flog.
"I'll jacket him when he comes in."

Jacketting, *m.* A hard day's work.

Jambreads, *m.* Slices of jam and bread.

Jaunce, *e.* A weary journey.
"I doänt justly know how far it is to Hellingly, but you'll have a middlin' jaunce before you get there."

January-butter, *e.* Mud. It is considered lucky to bring mud into the house in January.

Jawled-out, *w.* Excessively fatigued.

Jib, *e.* The under-lip. To hang the jib, is to look cross.

Jigger-pump, *e.* A pump used in breweries to force the beer into the vats.

Johnny, *m.* "Old Johnny" is one of the numerous names given to the ague.
"Old Johnny has been running his finger down my back."

A spider is considered a useful insect for the cure of the ague. If taken internally, it should be rolled up in a cobweb and swallowed like a pill. If applied externally, it should be placed in a nutshell and hung round the neck in a bag of black silk. The ague generally hangs about Sussex people a long time.

JOINT-STEDDLE, or JOINT-STOOL, *w.* A stool framed by joinery work, so called in distinction from stools rudely formed of a single block.

"Away with the joint-stools, remove the court-cupboard."
—*Romeo and Juliet*, Act i. sc. 5.

JORAM, *m.* A capacious bowl or goblet; called in Norfolk a Jeroboam.

JOSSING-BLOCK, *e.* A block by which a rider mounts his horse, often seen at the gate of a country churchyard in Sussex.

JOSS-UP, *e.* To mount a horse.

"Ah! she josses up like a feather, she doänt want no jossing-block nor chair either."

JOSTLE, *m.* To cheat.

JOUND, *m.* Joined.

"I jound in with them up at Burwash Wheel, and they jostled me out of ninepence."

JOY. A jay.

"Poor old Master Crockham, he's in terrible order, surelye! The meece have taken his peas, and the joys have got at his beans, and the snags have spilt all his lettuce."

JOURNEY, *m.* [*Journée*, French.] A day's work. This word is spelt in old parochial account-books jorney, but in such MSS. the spelling seems to have depended upon the taste or caprice of the writer.

JUB, *e.* To move slowly and heavily, like a sluggish horse.

JUB, *e.* A slow trot.

JUG. A nickname given to the men of Brighton.

JUMPING-BETTY, *e. Impatiens balsamina.*

JUMP-ROUND-AND-HANG-BY-NOTHING, *e.* To make haste.

"She's a capital good girl to work, she can jump round and hang by nothing, I can tell you."

JUMP-UP-AND-KISS-ME, *m.* The pansy. *Viola tricolor.*

JUNE-BUG, *m.* The green beetle.

A Dictionary of the Sussex Dialect.

JUSTABOUT, *m.* Certainly; extremely.

"I justabout did enjoy myself up at the Cristial Palace on the Foresters' day, but there was a terr'ble gurt crowd; I should think there must have been two or three hundred people a-scrouging about."

JUST-BEAST, or JOIST-BEAST, *e.* A beast taken in to graze.

This word is probably a corruption of agist-beast. Agistment was the feeding of cattle in a common pasture at a fixed price. In the year 1531 the agistment of a horse for the summer cost 3s. 4d.

JUSTLY, *m.* Exactly.

"I dŏànt justly know how old I be, but I knows I be above sixty years of age; for ye see I went to work when I was somewhere's about nine years old (that was in old Mus Ridge's time), and I kep on till I was somewheres about fower-and-twenty; and then a young woman got me into trouble, and I was forced to goo away to sea; but I didn't hold to that above six or seven years, and then I come home and got drawed for the Militia and sarved ten year, and then volunteered for a sodger and sarved my time fifteen years; and then I comed back to the farm, and there I've worked for fower-and-farty year, till I got quite entirely eat up with the rheumattics, and now I aint done naun for these last ten years, and sometimes they be better than what they be othersome; so I knows I be *above* sixty year old, though I dŏànt justly know how old I be."

K.

KEBLOCK, *w.* The wild turnip.

KEDDLE-NETS. Stake nets.

KEELER, *m.* [*Coélan*, Ang. Sax., to cool.] A shallow tub used for cooling beer.

KELL, *m.* [*Cyl*, Welsh.] A kiln.

"I've been quite out of kelter ever sen I've lived up aside of the lime-kells; the reek's enough to choke one otherwhiles."

KELLICK, *w.* A romp.

KELTER, *m.* Condition. "This farm seems in very good kelter."

Ken, *m.* [Corruption of Kin.]

Kerf, *w.* [Ang. Sax., *ceorfan*, to cut; *cyrf*, a cutting.] The cut made by a saw; a notch.

Kettle, *w.* A swelling; a dark lump found in suet or pork.

Kettly, *w.* Full of kettles or kernels.

Keveling, *m.* The name given at Brighton to the skate; at Hastings the fish is called "a maid," and at Dover "a damsel."

Kex, *e.* The dry hollow stalk of hogweed, cow parsley, and other umbelliferæ.

Kickel, *e.* [*Cicel*, Ang. Sax.] A sort of flat cake, with sugar and currants strewn on the top.

Kid, *e.* A small wooden tub.

Kid, *w.* The pod of peas or beans.

Kiddle, *e.* To entice; to coax.

Kiddle, *e.* [*Citelian*, Ang. Sax., to tickle.] To tickle.

"Those thunderbugs did kiddle me so that I couldn't keep still no hows."

Kiddle, *w.* Delicate.

Kilk, *m.* Charlock, *sinapis arvensis*, a weed with a yellow flower which grows among the corn.

The employment of children at kilk-pulling is a serious obstacle to education in the agricultural districts.

Kime, *m.* A weazel.

A lady who had been giving a lesson to a Sunday school class upon Pharoah's dreams, was startled to find that all the boys supposed that the fat and lean kine were weazels.

Kimmell, *m.* A tub used for salting meat.

Kind, *m.* Fat; doing well, said of beasts.

Kink, *m.* [*Kink*, Dutch, a twist in a rope.] To twist; entangle.

Kissing-gate, *w.* The same as a cuckoo-gate.

Kiss-me, *e.* The wild heartsease. *Viola tricolor.*

Kiver, *w.* A large shallow tub.

Knap. [*Cnæp*, Ang. Sax., top.] The top of a hill, or any piece of rising ground.

Knettar, *e;* or, **Knittle,** *w.* [*Cnittan*, Ang. Sax., to knit.] A string fastened to the mouth of a sack to tie it with.

KNOW, *m.* Used as a substantive for knowledge.
"Poor fellow, he has got no know whatsumdever, but his sister's a nice knowledgeable girl."

KNOWLEDGEABLE, *e.* Well-educated.

KNUCKER. [*Hnægan*, Ang. Sax.] To neigh or whinny.

L.

LADDER-TYING. Fastening the upper branches of the hop-plant to the pole, which is reached by women standing on ladders.

LADES. [*Ladan*, Ang. Sax., to load.] Rails which project round the top of a waggon to enable it to bear a greater load.

LADSLOVE. Southernwood.

LADYCOW. The ladybird.
It is held extremely unlucky to kill a cricket, a ladybird, a swallow, martin, robin redbreast, or wren.

LADY'S-SMOCK. *Convolvulus sepium.* The bindweed of the hedges.

LAG, or LEG, *w.* A long narrow marshy meadow, usually by the side of a stream.

LAINES. Open tracts of arable land at the foot of the Downs.

LAMBSTONGUE. *Plantago media.*

LAMENTABLE, *m.* Very.
This word seems to admit of three degrees of comparison, which are indicated by the accentuation, thus,—
Positive—Laméntable, as usually pronounced.
Comparative—Larméntable.
Superlative—Larmentààble.
"Master Chucks he says to me says he, ''tis larmentable purty weather, Master Crockham.' 'Larmentààble!' says I."

LANSCOT, or LANDSCOTE. The assessment of lands for the maintenance of the church. Now obsolete.

LAND, *m.* Low ground, especially arable land, as distinguished from the hill, used in the Southdown country.

LAPSY. Lazy; slow; indifferent.

LARDER. A gamekeeper's larder is the place where he nails up the weazles, stoats and vermin which he kills.

Larder, *m.* [Corruption of Ladder.]

"Master's got a lodge down on the land yonder, and as I was going across totherday-morning to fetch a larder we keeps there, a lawyer catched holt 'an me and scratched my face."

Lash, *m.* To get into a passion.

"He makes me lash and swear otherwhile when he be so lapsy; soonasever I'm backturned he's off after the birds-nestes, or up to some game or another."

Last, *e.* A last of herrings is ten thousand.

Last, *e.* A court of twenty-four jurats who levy rates for keeping up the marshes.

Lasus. A water meadow.

Lats. [*Latta*, Ang. Sax.] Laths.

Lattin, *w.* Plate-tin. Spelt lattyn in an inventory dated 1549, but in that year people spelt as they pleased.

Laurence. A mysterious individual whose influence is supposed to produce indolence. "Old Laurence has got hold of me" means "I have got a fit of idleness."

Lavant, *w.* [*Lafian*, Ang. Sax., to sprinkle with water; or, *Laver*, French, to wash.] A violent flow of water.

"How it did rain! It ran down the street in a lavant."

Lawyer, *e.* A long bramble full of thorns, so called because,

"When once they gets a holt an ye, ye doänt easy get shut of 'em."

Lay, *m;* or **Ley**. [*Leag*, Ang. Sax.] Land laid down for pasture; not permanently, but to be broken up every three or four years.

Laylock, *m.* The lilac tree.

Lay-up, *m.* To hide and lie in wait for any one.

Lean, *m.* Unprofitable.

"Ah, sir! stone-breaking's a lean job for those that aint used to it."

Lean-to, *m.* A shed constructed against the side of another building.

Leap, *e.* [*Leap*, Ang. Sax., a basket for catching fish.] A large deep basket.

Leap, *e.* Half-a-bushel. (See Seed-leap.)

Lear. Thin; hungry; faint.

LEARN. To teach.

"I'll lay-up for him one of these nights and leather him middlin' if I catches him; I'll learn him how to steal my apples, letbehow'twill."

LEASE, *m.* To glean.

LEASE-WHEAT, *m.* The ears of corn picked up by the gleaners.

LEAST. [*Loéstan*, Ang. Sax.] To last.

"I've picked up a little leasewheat, but that wont least very long; leastways not above a week or two."

LEASTWAYS. [Leastwise.] At least.

LEATHER. To flog.

LEAZE, *m.* The right of feed for a bullock or sheep on a common.

LEETLE. [Diminutive of Little.]

"I never see one of these here gurt men there's s'much talk about in the peapers, only once, and that was up at Smiffle Show adunnamany years agoo. Prime minister, they told me he was, up at Lunnon; a leetle, lear, miserable, skinny-looking chap as ever I see. 'Why,' I says, 'we döant count our minister to be much, but he's a deal primer-looking than what yourn be.'"

LENT. A loan.

"I thank you for the lent of your horse."

LETBEHOW'TWILL, *m.* An expression always pronounced as one word, meaning, let the consequences be what they may; abbreviated in West Sussex into behowtel.

LEW. [*Hleowth*, Ang. Sax., warmth.] Sheltered from the wind.

"My garden is nice and lew."

LEWTH. Shelter.

"You wont find but very little lewth on the hill."

LIBBET, *e.* A stick used to knock down fruit from the trees.

When throwing at cocks was a fashionable sport, the stick which was thrown had lead let in at the end, and was called a libbet.

"The old custom of throwing at cocks on Shrove Tuesday is said to date from the fact of the crowing of a cock having prevented our Saxon ancestors from massacreing their conquerors, another part of our ancestors, the Danes, on the morning of a Shrove Tuesday, when they were asleep in their beds."
—*Brand's Popular Antiquities.*

LIDDS, *m.* Large open fields.

LIGHTING. For lightning.
"There was a good deal of lighting last night."

LIKE. This word added to adjectives somewhat qualifies the force of their meaning.
"She seems so melancholy-like" means "she seems rather melancholy."

LINK. [*Hlinc*, Ang. Sax., a ridge of land.] A word used in the Southdowns for a green wooded bank, always on the side of a hill between two pieces of cultivated land.

LIONS MOUTH, *w.* Ground ivy. *Glecoma hederacea.*

LIP. [See Leap.] A wooden box of a peculiar shape, which is carried by the seedsman when sowing.

LIPPY, *m.* Impertinent; apt to answer saucily.

LIST, *m.* To leak.
"That new lean-to of yourn is a poor temporary thing; I reckon it wont least long, for the water lists through the roof already."

LITHER, *e.* Idle.

LITHER. Supple; lithy; pliable.

LITTEN. [*Líctún*, Sax.] A churchyard.

LITTER, *m.* Loose straw or anything thrown into a farmyard for cattle to lie upon and tread into manure.

LIVE, *e.* Real.
"She thinks she looks like a lady, but no one would take her for a live lady."

LIVERSICK. A hangnail on the finger.

LIZENED. Lean; shrunk, as applied to corn.

LOANST. A loan.
"Will you lend mother the loanst of a little tea."

LOCH.* The rut of a cart-wheel.

LODE.* [*Lád*, Ang. Sax., a way; a canal.] A drift-way, or cut for water; a ford.

LODGE, *m.* An outhouse; a shed.
"I found him here as melancholy as a lodge in a warren."
—*Much Ado About Nothing*, Act ii. sc. 1.

A Dictionary of the Sussex Dialect. 71

LODGE. [*Logian*, Ang. Sax.] To alight or fall on anything so as to remain there.

"My ball has lodged up on the window-sill."

LODGED. Corn or grass beaten down by wind and rain is said to be lodged.

 " We'll make foul weather with despised tears;
 Our sighs, and they, shall lodge the summer corn,
 And make a dearth in this revolting land."
 —*Richard II.*, Act iii. sc. 3.

LONESOME. Lonely; far from neighbours.

LONG-DOG, *m.* A greyhound.

LONG-PURPLES. The flowers of *orchis mascula*.

 " And long purples,
 That liberal shepherds give a grosser name."
 —*Hamlet,* Act iv. sc. 7.

LOOKER, *e.* [*Lócian*, Ang. Sax., to look.] A shepherd or herdsman; a man employed to look after cattle in the marshes.

LOOK-OUT, *e.* To open. Said of a window.

"It's no manner of use your trying; the window wont look out, for there was such a terr'ble big draught come in that father he took and made it fast."

LOPE-OFF. To go away in a secret, sly manner (probably connected with the word elope).

"The old dog was round here just now, but he must have loped off somewhere, he's gone off along with the shepherd very like."

LORDINGS, *e.* The best kind of fagots. The branches and tops taken off the wood which is being cut for hop-poles.

LOURDY.* [*Lourd*, French, dull.] Heavy; sluggish.

LURRY, *e.* A rapid, indistinct mode of reading.

LURRY, *e.* To hurry over work in a careless, slovenly manner.

LUSTY, *m.* Fat; in good order.

"You look as though what you've had sen' you was here last has done you good, you be got quite lusty!"

LUTON. A projection from a house, such as a bow window.

M.

Mad. Enraged.

"Ah! he just will be mad if he comes to hear an't."

Maid, *e.* This word is still sometimes used for children of both sexes who are too young to work.

"Words not a few were once applied to both sexes alike which are now restricted to the female, it is so even with girl, which once meant a young person of either sex."
—*Archbishop Trench, "English Past and English Present."*

Make or Mend, *e.* To interfere.

"He must go his own way, I'm not a-going to make or mend any more."

Malt-stirrer, *w.* A stick with sort of lattice work at the end, used for stirring the malt in brewing.

Mannered, *m.* A meadow abounding in sweet grasses is said to be good mannered.

"You wunt have such a very out-de-way gurt swarth, but 'tis countable purty mannered stuff, I call it."

Marchet, *w.* "Every widow holding by her bench is bound by the custom of the manor to pay unto the lord of the said manor, at the time of her next marriage after she is first a widow, her best beast of any manner of quick cattle, for and in the name of a Marchant, otherwise called a Marchet." —*Customs of the Manor of Bosham.*

Mare, *w.* A shallow lake.

Marestails. Streaky white clouds, said to indicate wind.

Martin, *e.* When a cow has two calves, one of which is a male and the other a female, the latter is called a free-martin, and it is supposed that she will always be barren.

Marvel. Hoarhound.

Mask. Completely covered with anything, but generally mud or blood.

"Why! you're one mask! Wherever have you been?"
"The boys shoved me into the masoner's mortar mixen."

Masoner, *m.* A bricklayer.

MASTER. (Pronounced Mass.) The distinctive title of a married labourer.

A single man will be called by his Christian name all his life long; but a married man, young or old, is "Master" even to his most intimate friend and fellow workmen, as long as he can earn his own livelihood; but as soon as he becomes past work he turns into "the old gentleman," leaving the bread-winner to rank as master of the household.

"Master" is quite a distinct title from "Mr.," which is always pronounced Mus, thus,—

Mus Smith is the employer.

Master Smith is the man he employs.

MASTER. The old custom of the wife speaking of her husband as her "master" still lingers among elderly people; but both the word and the reasonableness of its use are rapidly disappearing in the present generation.

It may be mentioned here that they say in Sussex that the rosemary will never blossom except where "the mistus" is master.

MASTERFUL. Overbearing.

MAUND. [*Mand*, Ang. Sax., a basket.] A hand basket with two handles.

MAUNDER, *e.* [*Maudire*, French, to curse.] To mutter or grumble.

MAUNDER. To wander about thoughtfully.

MAVIN.* The margin.

MAWKIN, *w.* A scarecrow.

MAXON, *m.* [*Meox*, Ang. Sax., dung.] A manure heap.

MAY-BE and MAYHAP. Perhaps.

"May be you knows Mass Pilbeam? No! doänt ye? Well, he was a very sing'lar marn was Mass Pilbeam, a very sing'lar marn! He says to he's mistus one day, he says, 'tis a long time, says he, sence I've took a holiday—so cardenly, nex marnin' he laid abed till purty nigh seven o'clock, and then he brackfustes, and then he goos down to the shop and buys fower ounces of barca, and he sets hisself down on the maxon, and there he set, and there he smoked and smoked and smoked all the whole day long, for, says he, 'tis a long time sence I've had a holiday! Ah, he was a very sing'lar marn—a very sing'lar marn indeed."

MAY-BUG, *m.* Cockchafer.

May-weed, *m.* *Anthemis cotula.*

Mead. [*Moéd*, Ang. Sax.] Still used for meadow.

Meal. [*Moél*, Ang. Sax., a fixed portion.] The quantity of milk taken from the cow at one milking.

Meece, *m.* Mice.

"The meece just have tarrified my peas."

Among other Sussex remedies it is said that a mouse roasted alive is good for the whooping-cough. Whether it is really good for the whooping cough or not I cannot say, but I am sure that it must be bad for the mouse.

Mend, *m.* To spread out manure (amendment) over a field.

Meresman, *m.* A parish officer who attends to the roads, bridges and water-courses.

Mersc. [*Mersc*, Ang. Sax.] A marsh.

Mesh, *m.* The Southdown folk always speak of Pevensey level as The Mesh.

"I went down to Pemsey last week, and walked out on The Mesh. Beautiful place, surelye! No hills, no trees, nor nothing to interrupt the view."

Messengers. Large white flying clouds, indicating rough weather.

Meuse, *w.* A hole through a hedge made by a rabbit or hare; an old French sporting term.

Mew. [*Méu*, Ang. Sax.] A seagull.

Middling. This word has many different meanings which are expressed by the tone of voice in which it is said.

It may mean very much, as, "He lashed out middlin', I can tell ye!"

Or it may mean tolerably well, as, "I doänt know but what she made out purty middlin'."

Or it may mean very bad, as, "How did the wedding go off?' 'Middling, thank you, sir.' 'What, only middling! wasn't it all right?' 'Why, no sir, not quite, for you see the parson he entirely forgot all about it, and he'd gone away, so we was forced to wait in church two hours.'"

Midge. [*Mycg*, Ang. Sax., a gnat.] All gnats are called midges in Sussex.

Miff. To give slight offence; to displease.

Mile-stones. The churches in the Downs are called Sussex mile-stones.

A Dictionary of the Sussex Dialect.

MILEMAS, *m.* [Corruption of Michaelmas.]

MILKMAIDS, *e.* The flowers of the *convolvulus sepium*.

MIND, *m.* [*Mynan*, Ang. Sax.] To remember.
"I minds him well, he was along here last Milemas."

MINNIS, *e.* A piece of rising ground.
One of the rocks on the East Hill, at Hastings, is called The Minnis Rock. In Kent the word is used for a high common.

MINTS. The mites in cheese, meal or flour.

MINTY. Full of mites.

MISAGIFT.* Misgiven; mistaken.

MISAGREE, *m.* To disagree.
"I doànt see how anyone can be off from misagreeing with these here people next door, for the old man's that miserable that he wont lend nothing to nobody, and the children be that mischieful that one doànt know where to be for 'em."

MISCHIEFUL, *m.* Full of mischief.

MISERABLE, *m.* Miserly; stingy.

MISHEROON. [*Mousseron*, French.] A mushroom.

MISLIKE. [*Mislícian*, Ang. Sax.] To dislike.
> "My lord of Winchester, I know your mind;
> 'Tis not my speeches that you do mislike,
> But 'tis my presence that doth trouble you."
> —II *Henry VI.*, Act i. sc. 1.

MISS. Abbreviation of mistress. The title of a married woman; single ladies being addressed as Mrs.

MISTUS. Is the usual pronunciation of mistress.
It is very difficult to say at what age a Sussex man's wife ceases to be his *mistus* and becomes *the old 'ooman*, and finally lapses (probably in her second childhood) into *the old gal*.

MISWORD, *m.* A cross, angry, or abusive word.
"I am sure my master's never given me a misword all the years we've been married."

MIXEN. [*Mixen*, Ang. Sax.] A heap of mixed manure.

MIZMAZE. Confusion.
"He came upon me so quick, and axed me so suddent, I was all of a mizmaze."

Moak. [*Max, masc*, Ang. Sax., a mesh, a noose.] The mesh of a net.

"Ordered, that no fisherman of the town should fish with any trawl net whereof the moak holdeth not five inches size throughout." —*Hastings Corporation Records*, 1604.

Mock-beggar-hall. A house which has an inviting external aspect, but within is poor and bare, dirty and disappointing. A farm near Rye bears this name.

Moil. Trouble; vexation.

Mole Plough, *w.* A draining plough.

Mommick, *m;* or **Mammick.** To cut or carve awkwardly or unevenly.

"Whether his fall enraged him, or how 'twas, he did so set his teeth and tear it; O, I warrant how he mammocked it!"
—*Coriolanus*, Act i. sc. 3.

Money-purse. A purse.

Monger. [*Mangere*, Ang. Sax., a dealer.] A man who has anything for sale.

A field at Selmeston is called The Monger's Plot.

Moonshine. Smuggled spirits.

Moonshiner. A beast that will not fat; a diseased beast that has to be driven off to the butcher's yard by night.

Morgan. May-weed. *Anthemis cotula.*

More. As big-more, or as long-more, means as big again, or as long again.

"'Tis as fur more from here to Hellingly as what it is from here to Hailsham."

Mort. [Icel., *Mart*, neuter of *margr*, many.] A great many.

"Yes, I've got a mort of children, but there's not one that's bringing in anything."

Mortacious. Mortal; very.

"My old sow's mortacious bad, surelye!"

Mortal. A term of reproach.

"What a young mortal that is; he's always at something!"

Mosey. Musty; soft; woolly.

Most-in-ginral, *m.* Generally.

"I most-in-ginral goos to church, but I goos to chapel otherwhile when 'tis so slubby."

A Dictionary of the Sussex Dialect.

Mother, *e.* To take care of.

"I doänt mind mothering the dog for you for a week or two."

Mothering. The service for the churching of women.

It is considered most unlucky for a woman after giving birth to a child to cross the high-road, or to pay a visit before she has been to church to return thanks.

Lupton, in his first book of notable things, ed. 1660, p. 49, says:—"If a man be the first that a woman meets after she comes out of the Church, when she is newly churched, it signifies that her next child will be a boy; if she meets a woman, then a wench is likely to be her next child. This is credibly reported to me to be true."

Mothering-pew. The pew reserved for women who desire to be churched.

It is on record that an elderly maiden lady once found her way by accident into the mothering pew in a strange church, and joined devoutly in the service, which included that appointed for the churching of women, but did not discover that she had herself been churched till the clerk handed her the alms-dish for her offering.

Mother-wo. A contraction of "come hither wilt thou." A carter's call to his horse.

Mothery. Mouldy; generally applied to liquor which has become thick and incrusted.

Mowburned, *m.* Hay which has fermented in the stack.

Muck, *m.* To hurry; to overwork.

"She's mucking about from morning to night."

Mucked-up. All in confusion.

"I doänt know as you'll find a seat, for we be all so mucked-up this morning."

Muck-grubber. A sordid miser. The sort of man who would search in the dung-heap or any filthy place for the sake of money.

Muck-out. To clean thoroughly.

"I doänt think that old house has been properly mucked-out for the last ten years."

Muddle-about. To do a little work.

"I'm ever so much better, and I shouldn't wonder but what I shall be able to muddle about in a day or two."

Mudgelly.* Broken, as straw is by being trodden by cattle.

Mum-chance, *m.* A stupid, silent fellow.

Mush, *e.* A marsh.
> "He's a stupid mumchance chap; seems as though he'd lived all his time down in the mush and never spoken to no-one."

Music. Any musical instrument.

N.

Nabble, *m.* To chatter; to gossip; to idle about.

Nabbler. A gossip.

Nail. A weight of eight pounds.
> "The hog weighed twelve nails."

Napery, *w.* [*Nappe*, French, a table cloth.] Linen, but especially table linen.

Narre, *w.* [*Knorren*, Dutch, to growl.] To growl like a dog.

Native. Birthplace; native place. Used as a substantive.
> "Heathfield is my native. I was borned at the cottage just beyond the pay-gate where there's postes beside the road."

Naughty-man's-plaything. Stinging nettle. *Urtica dioica.*

Naun, *m.* Nothing.

Naun-but. Only; answering to the northern expression nobbut.
> "I should have gone to Lewes market naunbut I hadn't got naun to take there."

Near, *m.* Stingy.

Neat. Exact; full; said of measurements, as "'Tis ten rod neat, no more nor no less."

Neb, *e.* [*Neb*, Ang. Sax., the bill or beak.] The pole of an ox-cart, or timber tug, so called from its shape.

Neb, *m.* The handle of a scythe.

Neighbour-together. To be good friends.

Neighbour's-fare, *e.* The same bad luck.
> "We've got neighbour's fare, for we've neither of us got an umbrella."

A Dictionary of the Sussex Dialect.

Nestle. To be restless.

Nestle-about, *m.* To work about a little in and out of the house.
 "I aint done naun but just nestle about house for the last three weeks, and I be quite nett-up this weather."

Nettle-spring. The nettle-rash.

Nett-up. Exhausted with cold.

News. To tell anything as news.
 "It was newsed about."

Nexdy. [Contraction of next day.] The day after to-morrow.

Ni, *w.* [*Nid*, French, a nest; spelt ni in old French.] A brood of pheasants.

Nidget, *e.* A little bug.

Nidget. A horse-hoe used for cleaning the ground between rows of hops, called in some parts of East Sussex an idget.

Niff. To quarrel; to be offended.

Nip, *e.* A stingy fellow; a close and sharp bargainer; just honest and no more.

Nipper, *m.* A common nickname for the youngest member of the family, or for one who is unusually small for his age.

Nod. The back of the neck.
 "It catched me right across the nod of my neck."

Nogging. Courses of bricks worked in between a frame of wood work in a building.

Nohows, *m.* In no way. Often expanded into "no-hows-de-wurreld," for no how in the world.

Nonce, *w.* Purpose; intent; design.
 "I have cases of buckram for the nonce, to immask our noted outward garments." —1 *Henry IV.*, Act i. sc. 2.

Non-plush. [Non-plus.] Completely bewildered.

No-one-wheres. Superlative form of nowhere.
 "I shouldn't have been no ways consarned about it, naunbut my mistus she took on so; she was quite non-plushed she was, for she couldn't find that young nipper no-one-wheres."

No-ought, *m.* "You had no-ought" is the same "as you ought not."

Norate, *m.* [Corruption of Orate; as nidget, from idget.] To talk officiously and fussily about other people's business.

"Master Norman he got nabbling over it, so it very soon got norated about all down the street."

Noration. An unnecessary publication of any piece of news or a secret.

"You have no-ought to have made such a noration about nothing, for you warn't no-ways consarned."

Nose-holes. Nostrils.

Not, *w.* [*Hnot*, Ang. Sax., shorn, cut.] Polled; said of sheep or cows without horns.

"Mus' Stapley he's been and bought some more of these here not-cows. I can't fancy them things no-hows-de-wurreld."

Notch. A run at cricket; so called from the custom in the country districts of reckoning the runs by notches cut in a stick.

Nottable, *m.* [*Notable*, French, remarkable.] Thrifty; industrious.

Mr. Lower says that this word is never applied in Sussex to a man.

"Mrs. Allbones she be a nottable 'ooman, surelye!"

Nover, *e.* High land above a precipitous bank.

No-ways. In no way.

Now-and-agin. Sometimes.

"I goos across the nover now-and-agin, but I mostly keeps to the road, for 'tis terrble nubbly for walking."

Nubbly, *e.* In lumps; full of small clods.

Nunting, *e.* Awkward looking.

Nunty, *e.* Dressed in a shabby or old-fashioned way.

Nunty, *m.* Sulky.

"Ye be middlin' nunty this marnin' seemingly; I doänt know naun what's putt ye out."

Nurt, *w.* To nurture; to train or bring up a child.

Nurt, *m.* To entice; to allure.

"He got linked-in with some chaps as wasn't no good, and they nurted him away, and he never come back nuther."

Nuther. [Corruption of Neither.]

O.

Oast-hair. A hair sieve used in oast-houses.

Oast-house. A place for drying hops.

With respect to the origin of this word, Mr. Durrant Cooper gives the following explanation,—

"As hops were introduced into England from Flanders, probably persons who understood the culture and cure of the article were brought with them; hence the word *heuse*, a house, was applied by these foreigners to the building where the hops were dried; subsequently *heuse* was corrupted into *haust*, or *oast*, and the word *house* very improperly appended by those who did not know the import of the original." —*Sussex Glossary*, pp. 63-64.

I think, however, that Rev. J. C. Egerton, of Burwash, has got nearer to the true derivation of the word. He informs me that, in Dutch, August is called oogst-maand, the harvest month, and tracing a connexion between oogst and oast, he is of opinion that oast-house is nothing more than oost-haus, the harvest-house, and that a close similitude may be found in the words August, août, oogst and oast.

With respect to this suggestion, Rev. W. W. Skeat considers that oogst is more likely to be connected with the Latin, Augustus, and that the meaning of harvest is quite secondary. He is of opinion that oost in oast-house is a mere corruption or dialectic variation of the Dutch eest, a drying kiln.

Obedience. [Obeisance.] A bow or a curtsey.

Ocklands, *m.* (See Hocklands.)

Oils, *w.* The beards of barley.

Old Clem. A figure dressed up with a wig and beard and pipe, and set up over the door of the inn where the blacksmiths held their feast in honour of their patron Saint on St. Clement's day (23rd November).

Old-father, *m.* The person who gives away the bride at her wedding.

Among the labouring classes in Sussex it is not the custom for the bride to be accompanied to church by her father. The bridal procession is very simple, and consists usually of four persons only—the bride and bridegroom, the bridesmaid, and the old father, who is usually the sweetheart of the bridesmaid if she is a single woman (which is not necessarily the case).

I was once marrying a shepherd who had arrayed himself in a very tight pair of white kid gloves; and suggested before the service began that he had better remove the glove from his right hand. "What!" he exclaimed, "Must I have her off? Then if she takes as long to come off as she did to putt on, we shan't get this here job over to-day."

OLD-MAN'S-NIGHTCAP. *Convolvulus sepium*.

ONE, *e.* To be at one, is to be consistent and determined.

ONE. To be one, is to be good friends; to be at two, is to quarrel.

OOD, *m.* [Corruption of Wood.]

OPEN, *m.* Not spayed; said of a sow.

ORATION. A fuss, not necessarily expressed by words.
"He makes such an oration about anything."

ORDER, *m.* Bad temper.
"He's in middlin' order, I can tell ye."

ORE, *e.* Seaweeds washed on shore by the tides.

ORNARY. [Corruption of Ordinary.] Inferior; unwell.

ORTS, *m.* Odds and ends; fragments of broken victuals.
"The fractions of her faith, orts of her love,
The fragments, scraps, the bits, and greasy reliques,
Of her o'er eaten faith, are bound to Diomed."
—*Troilus and Cressida*, Act v. sc. 2.

OTHERSOME. Some other.
"Sometimes my old gal's better than what she be othersome, but she be hem ornary again to-dee."

OTHERWHERES. Some other place.
"The King hath sent me otherwhere."
—*King Henry VIII.*, Act ii. sc. 2.

OTHERWHILE. Sometimes; occasionally.
"I has a horn of beer otherwhile, but never nothing to do me no hurt."

OUGHT, *m.* [See No-ought.]

OURN. Ours.

OUT-ASKED, or OUT-OF-ASK. To have had the banns published three times.

OUT-BOUNDERS, *w.* A word used in old parochial account books for ratepayers who pay rates in a parish where they do not reside.

OUT-STAND. To stand out against; to oppose and overcome.

"He wanted to have the calf for three pound ten, but I out-stood him upon that, for all that he was so set and contrairy."

OUT-DE-WAY, *m.* [Corruption of out of the way.]

"I never did see such tedious out-de-way larmentable poor ground in all my borns."

OVEN-RAKE, *e.* [*Ófenraca*, Ang. Sax.] A rake for clearing the ashes aside in a brick oven.

OVEN-SLICE, *w.* An iron shovel for taking the ashes out of the oven.

OVER, *e.* To cross over.

"You must over the bridge and keep straight on a-head."

OVERGET, *e.* To overtake.

OWLET, *m.* A moth.

OX-STEDDLE, *m.* Stabling or stalls for oxen.

Oxen are still used as draught-beasts; the Sussex breed being specially useful for the purpose. A team of eight oxen drawing a load is not an unusual sight in East Sussex, though it is not seen so frequently as it was twenty years ago.

OX-TIGHTS, *w.* Chains for use with oxen.

P.

PACKLED, *m.* Speckled.

PADDLE, *m.* To trample about in the wet and dirt.

PAINFUL. Painstaking.

There is an inscription on a brass in Selmeston Church, dated 1639, which commences thus,—

> The body of Henry Rogers,
> A painfull preacher in this church
> Two and thirty yeeres.

PAIR-OF-BARS, *w.* Rails made to lift out of the sockets, so as to admit of a cart passing through; called in East Sussex a bar-way.

PALLANT. [*Palent*, Ang. Sax., a palace.] The Pallant is a district of Chichester opening from the West-street.

Murray says "It forms a miniature Chichester with its own four streets, and is the *palatinate*, or Archbishop's peculiar."

PALM. The bloom of the willow, which is worn on Palm Sunday.

In Kent yew-trees are always called palms.

PANNAGE, *m.* The mast of the oak and beech on which swine feed in the woods.

A copyhold right to these existed in one of the manors of Brighton.

PANDLE, *m.* A shrimp. Also used in Kent.

PARGET. [Old English *pariet*, a wall; derived from the Latin *paries*.] To plaster with cement; especially to plaster the inside of a chimney with cement made of cow-dung and lime.

PARLY. [*Parler*, French, to talk.] To talk French, or to talk unintelligibly.

A fisherman said, "I can make shift to parly a bit myself, but deuce-a-bit can I make out when the Frenchies begins to parly me."

A maid servant being asked who was with her master, answered that she didn't rightly know, but she knew he was a *Parly-German!*

PARSON-ROOK. A Royston-crow.

This species has obtained the specific name given by the Romans to some bird of the crow kind, deemed of unlucky omen—*sinistra cornix*.

PARTIAL. To be partial to anything, means, to like it; generally in the sense of relishing.

"I be very partial to a few pandles."

PARTICULAR, *m.* To look particular, is to look unwell.

"He's been looking very particular for some time past."

PASSEL, *m.* [Corruption of Parcel.]

PASTIME, *m.* [Pass and time.] This word is used according to its original acceptation, not so much to express amusement, as occupation for the mind.

"I likes evening school, 'tis such a pastime; but there's a passel of chaps that comes and doänt want to learn naun themselves, and wunt let any one else."

PASSTIME, *m.* Time passed.

"He mustn't expect to get well all in a minute. I tell him there's no passtime for that yet."

PAT. A hog-trough.

PATHERY. Silly; applied to sheep which have the water on the brain.

PATTENS AND CLOGS, *e. Lotus corniculatus.* Also called pigs'-pettitoes, and ladies' fingers.

PAUL. [*Pal*, Ang. Sax., a stake.] A division of tenantry land at Brighton, usually containing about the eighth part of a tenantry acre.

PAY-GATE. A turnpike gate.

PEAKED, *m.* [*Piqué*, French.] Fretful; unwell.
"Weary seven nights, nine times nine,
Shall he dwindle, peak, and pine."
—*Macbeth*, Act i. sc. 3.

PEASHALM. [*Healm*, Ang. Sax., stubble.] Pea-straw.

PECK. A pick-axe.

PECK. To use a pick-axe.

These words illustrate the following evidence given by a witness in a case of manslaughter,—

"You see he pecked he with a peck, and he pecked he with a peck, and if he'd pecked he with his peck as hard as he pecked he with his peck, he would have killed he, and not he he."

PEEL, *m.* [*Pelle*, French, a shovel.] A wooden shovel with a long handle, used for putting the bread into the oven.

PEERT, *m.* Lively.

"She just is a nice pleasant peert young lady."

PEEZE. To ooze out; to leak.

PEG-AWAY. To eat or drink voraciously.

In ancient times the liquor was handed round in a wooden vessel, marked at different distances from the bottom with pegs; each drinker in his turn drank as much as would reduce the liquor down to the next peg below; hence, to peg away, is to drink fast, so as to lower the liquor in the vessel very quickly.

PELL. A hole of water, generally very deep beneath a waterfall.

A broad shallow piece of water, larger than an ordinary pond.

PELL, *e.* To wash away the ground by the force of water.

PEN, *m.* A stall for a horse in a stable.

PENNOCK. A little bridge over a water-course; a brick or wooden tunnel under a road to carry off the water.

PENNY-RATTLE, *w.* Yellow rattle. *R. crista Galli.*

PERCER, *w.* [*Perçer*, French.] A piercer; a punch used by blacksmiths.

PERK-UP. To toss the head disdainfully.
> "Verily
> I swear, 'tis better to be lowly born,
> And range with humble livers in content,
> Than to be perked-up in a glittering grief,
> And wear a golden sorrow."
> —*King Henry VIII.*, Act ii. sc. 3.

PERRAMBLE. [Corruption of Preamble.]
> "He set to and punched into him without any perramble whatsumdever."

PEST. A common ejaculation.
> "What the pest has become of the watering pot?"

PET, *m.* [*Pett*, Ang. Sax.] A pit.

PETTIGUES, *e.* Troubles; vexation.
> "She's not one as would tell her pettigues to everyone, but she's had as many as most for all that."

PETER-GRIEVOUS, *m.* [*Petit-grief*, French, little grief.] Fretful; whining.
> "What a peter-grievous child you are! Whatever is the matter?"

PHARISEES. Great uncertainty exists in Sussex as to the definition of this word according to its acceptation in the minds of country people, who always connect it with fairieses (their plural of fairy).

A Sussex man was once asked, "What is a pharisee?" and answered, with much deliberation and confidence, "A little creature rather bigger than a squirrel, and not quite so large as a fox," and I believe he expressed a general opinion.

Since writing the above, I find that polecats are called varies in Devonshire; so that possibly the person who gave this answer had been brought in contact with some west-country folk and had heard the word from them. It is not Sussex.

PICKÈD, or PIKED, *w.* Pointed.

PICKPOCKETS, *w.* Shepherd's purse. *Capsella bursa pastoris.*

PICK-UP. To overtake.
"I picked up the postman between Selmeston and Berwick."

PICKSOME. Dainty.

PICK-UPON. To annoy.
"They always pick upon my boy coming home from school."

PIGEON-COVE, *w.* A dove cot.

PIG-MEAT. Fresh pork. By the word pork alone, salt pork is always meant.

PIGSCOT, *w.* A pigstye.

PIKER. A gipsy or tramp.

PILLAR. A large thick pile of white clouds.

PILLOWBERE, *w.;* and PILLOWCOAT, *e.* A pillow case.

PILRAG, *e.* A field that has been ploughed up and neglected.

PIMPS, *m.* Small bundles of chopped wood for lighting fires.

PINNOLD, *e.* A small bridge. (See Pennock.)

PIPE-KILN, *w.* A framework of iron, in which long dirty clay pipes are put, and placed over a hot fire or in an oven, till they burn white and clean again.

PITCH, *e.* An iron stake for making holes in the ground for hurdles; called in West Sussex a folding bar.

PITCHER, *m.* The man who lifts and pitches the corn or hay up on to the wagon. Those who unload the wagons on to the stack or rick are called impitchers, or inpitchers.

PITHERED, *m.* Gummed-up.
"I've had such a terr'ble gurt cold, my eyes seem quite pithered-up o' mornings."

PIZE, *e.* A strong expression; thought by some to be connected with swearing by the pyx.
"What the pize have you got to do with it?"

PLAIN, *m.* Any piece of ground that is level, no matter how small it may be.

PLATE-BONE. The blade-bone.

Platty, *e.* Uneven; usually said of a crop.

To say that "apples are very platty this year" would mean that there is a quantity in some places and none at all in others.

Plaw, *e.* A small wood; a plantation.

Plog. To clog or hinder.

Pluck, *e.* The lungs, liver and heart of a sheep or lamb.

Plum-heavy. A small round cake made of pie-crust, with raisins or currants in it.

Dr. J. C. Sanger, of Seaford, when Government Surgeon at the Cape of Good Hope, was sent for to see an English settler. Reaching the house at tea-time, he joined the family at their meal, and on sitting down to the table he said, "You come from Sussex." "Yes," was the answer, "from Horse-mouncies (Hurstmonceux), but how did you know that?" "Because you have got plum-heavies for tea," said the doctor, "which I never saw but when I have been visiting in Sussex."

Poach, *m.* [*Pocher*, French, to thrust; poke.] To tread the ground into holes, as cattle do in wet weather.

"Mus' Martin's calves got into our garden last night; there was fowerteen 'an 'em, and they've poached the lawn about middlin' I can tell ye! Master will be mad!"

The word poacher evidently has the same derivation; the sportsman regards his game as his own, but the poacher intrudes, or pokes into the property of another, as explained in Cotgrave.

People frequently talk of poached eggs, as if they had been stolen, instead of delicately cooked (as they ought to be) in poches or bags of wire or muslin.

Poad-milk, *e.* The first milk given by cows after calving.

Pod. The body of a cart.

Pointing-stethe, *w.* A small anvil, or stithy.

Poison-berry, *w.* Black bryony. *Tamus communis*.

Poke, *w.* [*Pocca*, Ang. Sax., a pouch.] A long sack.

"To buy a pig in a poke" means to buy it in the sack and so to take a thing for granted without proper enquiry.

Pole-puller. The man whose business it is to pull the hop-poles out of the ground and lay them down for the pickers.

A Dictionary of the Sussex Dialect.

In former times, at the commencement of the hop-picking season, the pickers purchased a neck-cloth for the pole-puller. The article was of some showy colour, to make him more conspicuous in the hop-garden, and its purchase seems to have been attended with some convivialities, if we may judge from the following extract from the diary of Mr. Turner,—

"September 23, 1756.—Halland hop-pickers bought their pole-pullers nick-cloth and, poor wretches, many of them insensible."

POLLARD. The refuse siftings of flour, finer than bran and coarser than sharps.

POLT, *e.* A hard driving blow. The form *pult* occurs in early English.

POND-PUDDING. Another name for the Black-eyed Susan.

POOCH. (See Poach.) To push or dig into anything.

POOCHER, *m.* An instrument used by thatchers.

POOK-HALE. Puck's Hall; the fairy's cottage.

A cottage at Selmeston goes by this name, and one of our numerous ghosts is still said to frequent the spot.

There are many farms and closes in Sussex which owe their names to having been the reputed haunt of fairies.

POOR. Thin. The proverb "as poor as a church mouse" is connected with this meaning of the word. When the numerous candles which adorned the altar, or were placed before shrines of patron Saints, were removed at the Reformation, the mice which formerly frequented the churches were starved out.

POPPLE, *e.* To bubble. A poppling sea is when the waves rise and fall with a quick sudden motion.

POSNET, *w.* A skillet; a small saucepan.

POT-HANGER, *w.* A hook shaped like the letter s on which the black pot was hung over the fire to boil.

POUD.* An ulcer; a boil.

POULTS, *w.* Beans and peas sown and harvested together.

POUND, *m.* [Ang. Sax. *púnd*, a fold; *pyndan*, to pen up.] A small enclosure. A pigstye is called a hog-pound.

POUNTLE, *w.* Honest; reliable. [Probably a corruption of Punctual.]

POWDERING-TUB, *m.* A tub for salting meat.
> "From the powdering tub of infamy,
> Fetch forth the lazar kite of Cressid's kind."
> —*King Henry V.*, Act ii. sc. 1.

PRATT, *w.* The bar of a plough to which the traces are fastened.

PRAYERS-GOING, *e.* Service in church.
> "We only have prayers-going once on a Sunday at our church."

PRAYING-BOOK, *e.* The Prayer Book.

PRENSLEY, *m.* [Corruption of Presently.]

PRIMED. Half tipsy; overcharged with drink and ready to explode into any kind of mischief.

PRINT-MOONLIGHT, *e.* Very clear moonlight.
> "He *must* have been primed to fall into the pond such a night as that was, for t'was print-moonlight."

PROG. A linch-pin.

PRONG, *m.* A hayfork with two speens.

PROPER. Thorough.
> "He's a proper old rogue!"

PUCKER. A fuss. Over-anxiety, with a little touch of ill-temper.

PUCKERED-UP, *m.* Shrivelled up with cold.

PUCKETS.* Nests of caterpillars.

PUDDING-CAKE. A composition of flour and water boiled; differing from a hard dick in shape only, being flat instead of round.

PUG. A kind of loam.

PULL. To summon before the magistrates.

PUMPLE-FOOTED. Club-footed.

PURTY. [Corruption of Pretty.]

PURVENSION. Responsibility.
> "It is none of my purvension" means "I am not answerable for it."

PUTT-IN. To bury.
> "Master Hackleford is a man I always respacted, and if I knowed when he was a-going to be putt-in, I'd goo for sartin."

Q.

Quaint. [For acquainted.]

Quality, *w.* This word occurs in old parochial account books for a kind of tape.

Quartering, *w.* The wooden framing of a house, the upper story of which is made of wood-work covered with tiles.

Queer, *m.* To puzzle.
"It has queered me for a long time to find out who that man is; and my mistus she's been quite in a quirk over it. He döant seem to be quaint with nobody, and he döant seem to have no business, and for all that he's always to and thro', to and thro', for everlastin'."

Quern, *w.* [*Cwéorn,* Ang. Sax., a mill.] A hand-mill to grind malt.
"Are you not he
That frights the maidens of the villag'ry,
Skim milk, and sometimes labour in the quern?"
—*Midsummer Night's Dream,* Act ii. sc. 1.

Quest, *e.* To give tongue like a hound.

Quick, *w.* Pregnant.
"Faith, unless you play the honest Trojan, the poor wench is cast away; she's quick."
—*Love's Labour Lost,* Act v. sc. 2.

Quick. [*Cwic,* Ang. Sax., living.] Alive.
"I thought that the sheep was dead when I first saw it, but I found it was quick still."

Quick. To hurry; used actively and reflexively.
"I'll quick him fast enough if he doesn't quick himself a little more."

Quick. An expression applied to the sands when they are insecure from not being sufficiently firm and dry.
"You should not ride on the sands so soon after the tide has turned, for they are sure to be quick and shifting."

Quid. A cud.

Quiddy, *e.* [*Que dis tu?* French.] What do you say?
"Quiddy? I didn't hear what you said."

Quilers, or **Quoilers,** *w.* Part of the harness of a cart horse; the breeching.

Quiler-harness, *w.* The trace-harness.

Quill, *w.* A spring of water. (Variation of Well.)

Quilly, *m.* The roughness of the skin produced by cold, sometimes described as goose-flesh.

Quilt. To claw and pound with the paws, as cats do upon a carpet; also called "making bread." When the cat makes bread it is a sign of rain.

Quirk, *m.* A fuss; a whim; a fancy.

> "I may chance have some odd quirks and remnants of wit broken on me, because I have railed so long at marriage . . . When I said I should die a batchelor, I did not think I should live till I were marry'd." —*Much Ado About Nothing*, Act ii. sc. 3.

Quont. [Compare *contus*, Latin.] A barge-pole.

Quotted. Satiated; glutted.

R.

Rabbits, *e.* An ejaculation.
"What the rabbits! Why, its never you out in such weather as this, surelye!"

Rabbit's-meat, *m.* Wild parsley. *Anthriscus sylvestris.*

Racketting-riddle, *w.* [*Hriddel*, Ang. Sax., a sieve.] A cane-bottomed sieve.

Rackon, *m.* [Corruption of Reckon.]
"The fire burns middlin' rash; I rackon 'tis because 'tis so frosty."

Rack-up. To supply horses with their food for the night.

Rad. [Corruption of Rod.] The shaft of a cart; a measure of $16\frac{1}{2}$ feet, by which distance is more frequently measured than by yards, as elsewhere.

Raddles. [Diminutive of Rod.] Long supple sticks of green wood interwoven between upright stakes to make a hedge.

Raddle and Dab. Frame-work of timber filled in with mortar.

Raddle-fence, *e.* A hedge made with raddles.

Rades, *w.* The rails of a wagon.

A Dictionary of the Sussex Dialect.

RADICAL, *e.* Tiresome; disobedient.

"He's that radical that I doänt know whatever 'll become an him. I've told him adunnamany times not to ride on the rads, but 'tis no use what you says to him."

RAFTY, *e.* Very.

RAFTY, *w.* Ill-tempered; difficult to manage.

RAGGED-JACK, *w.* Scotch kale.

RAGGED-JACK, *e.* Ragged robin. *Lychnis flos-cuculi.*

RAKE, *e.* The sea is said to rake when it breaks on the shore with a long grating sound.

RAKE. "As lean as a rake" is a common proverb among Sussex people, who use the word in the same sense as in the following passage,—

"Let us revenge this with our pikes, ere we become rakes; for the gods know, I speak this in hunger for bread, not in thirst for revenge."
—*Coriolanus*, Act i. sc. 1.

"As lene was his hors as is a rake."
—*Chaucer*, Prol. l. 287.

RAMP, *e.* To grow rapidly and luxuriantly.

RAP-AND-RUN, or RAP-AND-REND.* [Icel, *hrapa*. To rush headlong.] To seize and plunder; to seize hold of everything one can.

RAPE. [*Hreppr*, Icelandic.] A division of a county comprising several hundreds.

The Normans divided the county of Sussex into six rapes—Hastings, Pevensey and Lewes, in East Sussex; Bramber, Arundel, and Chichester, in West Sussex. Each of these rapes had a castle near the coast, and an available harbour at its southern extremity, and formed what was called "a high road to Normandy."

RARE, *m.* [*Hrére*, Ang. Sax., raw.] Underdone.

RASH. [*Ræsc*, Ang. Sax., a flash.] Fierce and clear; said of a fire in frosty weather.

"His rash fierce blaze of riot cannot last,
For violent fires soon burn out themselves."
—*Richard II.*, Act ii. sc. 1.

RATHE.* Early; as rathe in the morning. (Ray.)

RATHER-RIPE. [*Hræth*, Ang. Sax., early.] The name of an apple which ripens early.

RATTLEBONE. Worn out; tumbling to pieces.

RANK. Smoke.

RAVE-CART. A common cart fitted with raves.

RAVES. Two frames of wood which are laid on the top of a wagon in such a way as to meet in the middle and project on all sides beyond the body of the vehicle, so as to enable it to carry a larger load.

REAFE. [*Redfian*, Ang. Sax., to seize; seize upon.] To anticipate pleasure; to long for the accomplishment of anything; to speak continually on the same subject.

REARING-FEAST. A feast given to the workmen when the roof is reared or put on the house.

REBELLIOUS. [Corruption of Bilious.]
"I should be very much obliged for a few of them rebellious pills."

RECKON, *m.* To suppose. A Sussex man uses the expression, "I reckon" as often as an American uses "I guess."

"Did put the yoke upon us; which to shake off,
Becomes a warlike people, whom we reckon
Ourselves to be." —*Cymbeline*, Act iii. sc. 1.

RECOLLECTS, *e.* Memory.
"I quite lost my recollects, and the doctor he redeemed it was through along of the fever."

REDEEM, *m.* [Corruption of Deem.] To consider; to give an opinion.

REEK, *m.* [*Redc*, Ang. Sax., smoke.] Fog or mist rising from the marsh.
"You common cry of curs! Whose breath I hate
As reek of the rotten fens."
—*Coriolanus*, Act iii. sc. 3.

REEVE. [*Ge-réfa*, Ang. Sax.] A bailiff; an officer of the lord of the manor.

REFUGE, *e.* To separate the inferior sheep or lambs from the flock.

REFUGE. [Corruption of Refuse.] Worthless; unsaleable.

RENDER. To give the finishing coat of plaster to a wall.

REVE, or REVES, *m.* Rent or tithes. The fishermen at Brighton are liable to pay six mackerel as reves each time they return from mackerel fishing.

REYNOLDS. "Mus Reynolds" is the name given to the fox.
When I was first told that "Mus Reynolds come along last night" he was spoken of so intimately that I supposed

A Dictionary of the Sussex Dialect.

he must be some old friend, and expressed a hope that he had been hospitably received. "He helped hisself," was the reply; and thereupon followed the explanation, illustrated by an exhibition of mutilated poultry.

RHEUMATTICS. A woman once said to me, "There's so many new complaints now-a-days to what there used to be; there's this here rheumatism there's so much talk about. When I was a gal 'twas the rheumattics, and I doànt know as there's much odds in it now—naun but if you wants to cure the rheumatism you wants a lot of doctor's stuff; but for my part, if ever I be troubled with the rheumattics (and I be quite eat-up otherwhile) I goos out and steals a tater, and carries it in my pocket till the rheumattics be gone."

RIB-LADE, *w.* The bar on the side of a wagon parallel with the lade.

RICE, *w;* RICE-HEADING, *e.* [*Hrís*, Ang. Sax., a twig.] Underwood cut sufficiently young to bear winding into hedges or hurdles.

RICKSTEDDLE, *m.* [*Hreac* and *Stéde*, Ang. Sax., a rick place.] An enclosure for corn or hay ricks.

RICKSTEDDLE, *w.* A wooden frame placed on stones on which to build the ricks.

RIDDER, *e.* [*Hridder*, Ang. Sax.] An oblong coarse wire sieve used with a blower for winnowing corn, the ridder being moved to and fro on a stake in front of the blower.

RIDDLE, *w.* [*Hriddel*, Ang. Sax.] A large sieve for sifting wheat in a barn.

RIDE, *m.* Any bridle-road, but generally a green way through furze or wood-land.

RIDE, *e.* A rut, or wheel mark.

RIDE, *m.* To be a burden.

"I didn't want to ride the club, so I declared off."

RIDE-HORSE, *e.* A saddle-horse.

RIDES, *e.* The iron hinges on a gate by which it is hung to the post and so swings or rides.

RIDGE-BAND, *e;* or RIDGE-STAY, *w.* [*Hryg*, Ang. Sax., the back.] That part of the harness which goes over the saddle on the horse's back, and being fastened on both sides, supports the shafts of the cart.

RIDGE-BONE. The weather boarding on the outside of wooden houses, common in Sussex and Kent.

Rife, *w.* A ditch on the moorland. (See Rythe.)

Ringle. [Diminutive of Ring.] A small ring, such as that put into the snout of a pig to prevent him from rooting up the floor of his sty.

  I find among the manorial customs the following regulation,—"It is also ordained that every one do yoke or ring his hogs before the feast of St. Michael the Archangel next, and the same keep so yoked or ringed until the feast of St. John the Baptist then next following, under pain of forfeiting to the lord, for every hog, for every week, 3s. 4d."

Ringle, *m.* To put rings in hogs' snouts.

Rip. To reap. The sickle is called the rip-hook.

Ripe. [*Ripa*, Latin.] A bank or sea-shore.
  A village in East Sussex is called by this name.

Ripiers. [Icel., *hrip*, a basket.] Men from the coast who carry baskets of fish to inland towns and villages. The word rip is still used in Scotland for a basket.

Rising, *e.* Yeast.

Robbut. [Corruption of Rabbit.] Sometimes pronounced as broadly as robert.

  "Robbuts! Ah, I lay you never see such a plààce for robbuts as what ourn is! I never should have beleft, without I'd seen 'em in my garden, that there was so many robbuts in the wurreld. Why they be ready to eat us up alive!"

Roke. [*Roec*, or *Reác*, Ang. Sax., smoke.] Steam; mist.

Romney-marsh. There is a saying in East Sussex that the world is divided into five parts—Europe, Asia, Africa, America, and Romney-marsh.

Rooster. The common cock. The Americans invariably call cocks by this name.

Rookery, *m.* A disturbance; a fuss and chattering.
  "I never knew of a wedding but what the women-folks made a middlin' rookery over it."

Rossel-fence, *w.* The same as raddle-fence.

Rother, *w.* [*Hryther*, Ang. Sax.] A horned beast.

Rough. Passionate; angry.
  "Mus Moppet he'll be middlin' rough if he sees you a throwing at he's rooster."

Roundel. A circle; anything round.

ROUND-FROCK. A loose frock or upper garment of coarse material, generally worn by country-people over their other clothes. A white round frock is considered mourning, and when worn (as I have sometimes seen it) under a great coat, the effect is by no means good, particularly when viewed from behind.

ROUPEY. [Connected with the Ang. Sax., *hrépan;* or the Icelandic, *hrópja*, to scream out.] Hoarse.

ROWENS, *m;* or ROUGHINGS, *e.* The latter grass which comes after mowing, and is frequently left for cattle to eat in the winter when it becomes coarse and rough.

RUBBER. The stone used for whetting the scythe.

RUBBIDGE. Rubbish; especially weeds in a garden.

RUDY, *m.* Rude.
"They boys! They boys! They be so rudy."

RUE, *w.* [*Rue*, French, a street.] A row; a hedge-row.

RUNAGATE. A good-for-nothing fellow.
"There let him sink, and be the seas on him!
White-livered runagate, what doth he there?"
—*Richard III.*, Act iv. sc. 4.

RUNDLET. A small circle. [Diminutive of Roundel.]

RUNT, *w.* To grub up the roots of trees by drawing them out of the ground in a way which does not much disturb the soil.

RUSTY, *w.* Unruly; ill-humoured.

RYTHE, *w.* [*Rithe*, Ang. Sax., a fountain; well; rivulet.] A small stream; usually one occasioned by heavy showers of rain.

S.

SABBED. Wet; saturated; sopped. (See Sape.)

SAD. Sodden; heavy; said of bread which has not risen well.

SAFE, *w.* Sure; certain.
"He's safe to be hanged."

Sag. [Connected with *Saégan*, Ang. Sax., to cause to descend.] To fit badly; to hang down on one side; to subside by its own weight or an overload.

> "The mind I sway by, and the heart I bear,
> Shall never sag with doubt, nor shake with fear."
> —*Macbeth*, Act v. sc. 3.

Salimote, *m.* The court of the lord of the old manor of Brighthelmston in 1656 was described as the Salimote Court.

Sallet. A salad. (As ballet for ballad.)

> "Sunday, May 13, 1764. Myself, Mr. Dodson and servant at church in the morn. We dined on a calf's heart pudding, a piece of beef, greens and green sallet. Mr. Hartley came to bring me a new wigg. Paid him in full for a new wigg £1. 15s., and new-mounting an old one, 4s."
> —*Diary of Mr. Turner, of East Hoathly.*

Shakespeare uses the word,—

> *Clown.*—"Indeed, sir, she was the sweet marjoram of the sallet; or, rather, the herb of grace."
> *Lafeu.*—"They are not sallet herbs you knave, they are nose herbs."
> —*All's Well that Ends Well*, Act iv. sc. 5.

Sally, *e.* [*Salig*, Ang. Sax.; *Salix*, Latin.] A willow.

Salts, *e.* Marshes near the sea, overflowed by the tides.

Sape. [*Sæp*, Ang. Sax.] Sap.

Sare. [*Searian*, Ang. Sax., to dry.] Withered; dry; said of wood. (See Sear.)

> "Burn ash-wood green,
> 'Tis fire for a Queen;
> Burn ash-wood sare,
> 'Twool make a man swear."

Sarment. A sermon.

> " I likes a good long sarment, I doos; so as when you wakes up it aint all over."

Sattered, *m.* Thoroughly soaked. (Probably a corruption of Saturated.)

Sauce, *m.* (Pronounced Sass.) Vegetables; but generally used of cabbages. The Americans speak of garden-sass.

> "I reckon I shään't have no sass at all this year, all through along on account of the drythe."

Saye. Serge or woollen cloth. —*Cheeseworth Inventory,* 1549.

Scad, *m.* A small black plum which grows wild in the hedges.

Scaddle, *m.* [*Scæthig,* Ang. Sax., hurtful.] Wild; mischievous; thievish. The Anglo-Saxon word *sceatha* has the same double meaning (1) a robber; thief; (2) an adversary.

Applied to a truant boy, or a cow which breaks through hedges, or a cat which steals.

Scade. Harm; mischief.

Scaly, *w.* Inclined to steal.

Scamble, *w.* To make a confusion of anything.

"The scambling and unquiet time
Did push it out of further question."
—*King Henry V.*, Act i. sc. 1.

Scar, *e.* [Possibly connected with Icel., *skár*, open, exposed.] Exposed to.

"Our house lays quite scar to the sea."

Scarcey, *m.* Scarce. Also used in Kent.

Scoring-axe. An axe used to chip round the stem of a tree, previous to falling (*i.e.*, felling it).

Sconce. [*Schans*, Dutch, a sconce.] A socket fixed in a wall for holding a candle.

Scorse. To exchange. Like scrunch for crunch, this word is corruption of the Old English word corse, which means to barter, exchange, &c.

"This catel he got with okering,
And spent al his lif in corsing."

i.e., "This cattle he acquired by usury, and led all his life in bargaining." —*Old Metrical Homilies.*

Spenser also uses the word,—

"And therein sat an old old man, half blind,
And all decrepit in his feeble corse,
Yet lively vigour rested in his mind,
And recompenst them with a better scorse;
Weak body well is changed for minds redoubled forse."
—*The Faerie Queene*, Book II., Cant. ix. 55.

The following instance will illustrate the modern use of the word,—

A gipsy boy, with whom I was on friendly terms, used to travel about this part of the country selling trumpery brooches and ornaments. As he was one day exhibiting the contents of his basket, I was surprised to see half-a-dozen onions loose among the jewelry. "What," I said, "do you sell onions, too?" "No, sir," he replied, "but I scorsed away a pair of diamond ear-rings for these few onions, with a lady down at the cottage yonder."

SCRATCH-ALONG. To pull through hard times.

"What with otherwhiles a day's turmut-hoeing, and otherwhiles a day's tan-flawin', and otherwhiles a job of gardenin', I've just managed to scratch along somehows."

SCRAZE. [Connected with graze.] To scratch, or rather to scratch and bruise at the same time.

"She was climmin' up after some scads and fell down and scrazed her knees."

SCRIER, or SCREER, *e.* A high-standing sieve which is used for cleansing corn from dust and other rubbish; sometimes called a screen.

SCROW, or SCROWSE, *e.* [Connected with the Old English word crus, wrathful.] Angry; dark and scowling.

SCRUMP, *e.* [*Scrimmian*, Ang. Sax., to wither up.] Anything undersized.

In Hampshire a small shrivelled up apple is called a scrumpling.

SCRY, *e.* To sift corn through a scrier.

SCUD. Driving rain; mist.

SCUFFLE, *e.* An outer garment worn by children to keep their clothes clean; a coarse apron for dirty work.

SCUFFLE-PLOUGH, *w.* A skim; a horse-hoe.

SCUPPIT. A wooden shovel used by maltsters and hop-driers.

SCUTCHETT,* *w.* The refuse of wood.

SCUTTY, *m.* A wren; also called a cutty.

The Sussex small boys have a Small Birds Act of their own, which is found sufficient for the protection of all birds which they consider entitled to protection, and commands much more respect and obedience than a recent Act of Parliament.

"Robins and wrens
Are God Almighty's friends;
Martins and swallers
Are God Almighty's scholars."

SEAM. [*Seam*, Ang. Sax.] Eight bushels, or a horse load.

SEAN, or SEINE. [*Seine*, Old French, still used in France.] A very large net used for catching mackerel or herrings.

SEAR. [*Searian*, Ang. Sax., to dry up.] Dry; withered; burnt up by the sun. (See Sare.)

" My May of life
Is fallen into the sear, the yellow leaf."
—*Macbeth*, Act v. sc. 3.

Season, *m*. Ground in good condition.

See. Used always as the perfect for saw.

"I never see such larmentable poor ground as this here. I've been diggin' it over to get a season to plant a little onion seed, but I shan't make naun an't."

Seed-cord.* [Connected with the Dutch word *korf*, a basket.] A wooden vessel in which the sower carries the seed.

Seed-lip, *m*. [*Sæd-leap*, Ang. Sax.] A basket for seed; a seed-cord.

Seedsman, *m*. The foreman of the farm, whose business it is to sow.

Sen. Since.

The Sussex word is the older form, and is traced to the Ang. Sax. *siththan*, which became *sin*, *sen*, or *sithen*, from the last of which was formed *sithens*, whence since.

"I haven't been over to Selmeston not sen I was seedsman at Muş Allwork's. Ah! he was a set sort of a man, he was, and no mistake."

Sessions. A great deal of business; a fuss.

"There's always such sessions over lighting up the church in winter time."

Set. Obstinate; self-willed; determined.

Set-out. A disturbance.

"There's been a pretty set-out up at the forge."

Settle. [*Setl*, Ang. Sax., a seat.] A wooden seat with a back and arms.

"He fell down off the settle and scrazed his nose and made as much set-out as though he'd been killed."

Severals, *m*. Portions of common assigned for a term to a particular proprietor; the other commoners waiving for a time their right of common over them.

"My lips are no common, though several they be."
—*Love's Labour Lost*, Act ii. sc. 1.

Ayscough gives the following note on this passage:—
"This word (several), which is provincial, means those fields which are alternately sown with corn, and during that time are kept several or severed from the field which lies fallow and is appropriated to the grazing of cattle, not by a fence, but by the care of the cowherd or shepherd, and in which the town bull only is allowed to range unmolested."

SEW, *e.* [*Sychu*, Welsh, to dry up; cognate with Latin *siccare.*] To drain land.

SEW, *e.* An underground drain.

SEW, *w.* A cow is said to be gone to sew when her milk is dried off.

SHACKY. Shabby; ragged.

SHACKLE, *w.* To idle about; to waste time; to be very busy about nothing.

SHADE. [*Shard.*] A piece of broken tile or pottery.

SHAG, *w.* A cormorant.

"As wet as a shag," is a common expression, taken from the idea of a cormorant diving frequently under the water.

SHARD, *e.* A gap in a hedge. This word, like shade, is derived from the Anglo-Saxon sceard, which means (1) a sherd; (2) a division.

SHARP.* The shaft of a cart.

SHARPS. The finest refuse siftings of flour. (See Pollard.)

SHATTER, *m.* A number or quantity.

"There's a tidy shatter of hops this year."

SHAUL, or SHAWLE. A wooden shovel without a handle, used for putting corn into a winnowing machine. This word is a variation of shool or shovel.

"I, said the owl,
With my spade and showl."

SHAW, *e.* A small hanging wood.

Ray defines it as "a wood that encompasses a close."

SHAY. A faint ray of light. In Kent the word means a general likeness, and seems to correspond to the Sussex bly.

A man who was trying to describe to me a fearful apparition which he had seen in Firle park, said, after much cross-examination, that it passed quite close to him in the form of an enormous white horse, and there was a bluish shay. I should myself have supposed that a horse and shay was a sufficiently common object of the country not to have excited undue influence, but on this occasion the appearance was so overwhelming that the man was ill for several days.

SHEAR, *e.* A spear, as an eel-shear.

SHEAT, *e.* A young hog of the first year. (See Shoot.)

SHEEP-CAGE. A framework out of which the sheep eat their hay, &c., in a strawyard.

SHEER. [*Scir*, Ang. Sax., clear, white.] Smooth and shiny, as flesh which is swollen.

SHEERES. The true Sussex man divides the world into two parts. Kent and Sussex forms one division, and all the rest is "The Sheeres." I have heard China and Australia both described as in the sheeres; but I confess that I was somewhat startled at being told that I was myself "a man as was well acquaint with the sheeres, and had got friends in *all parts* of this world and the world to come." This statement was meant as a compliment, but when I came to consider it afterwards, I was not sure that it was altogether complimentary to some of my friends.

SHEERE-MAN. A man who comes from the shires (and not necessarily sure of a favourable reception in Sussex).

SHEERE-MOUSE. A field mouse. A shrew-mouse.

The country people have an idea that the harvest-mouse is unable to cross a path which has been trod by man. Whenever it attempts to do so it is said to be immediately struck dead. This accounts (they say) for the numbers which on a summer's evening may be found lying dead on the edge of the field footpaths without any wound or apparent cause of death.

SHEERE-MOUSE. An epithet of derision applicable to a sheere-man. The phrase "the sheeres" is found in many other parts of England, and is generally expressive of a certain degree of depreciation. In Shropshire the manufacturing districts are spoken of as "down in the shires."

SHEERE-WAY, *e.* A bridle-way.

SHELL-FIRE. Phosphorescent light from decaying matter; called also fairy sparks.

SHELVE, *e.* To throw manure out of a cart by raising the fore-part so that the bottom may shelve or slope.

SHIM. [*Schim*, Dutch, a shade or ghost.] A glimpse of anything.

"I thought I saw a shim of the carpenter going by the gate just now, but I'm not sure."

SHIM, *e.* A narrow strip or glimpse of white on a horse's face.

SHIM. A horse hoe for cleaning the ground between rows of beans or hops.

SHIMPER. [*Scímian*, Ang. Sax., to shine or shimmer.] To shine brightly.

SHINGLES. Small wooden tiles made of split oak, used for roofs, steeples, &c.

There are several church spires in Sussex covered with these shingles.

SHIP, *m.* Sheep.

Seldom used in the singular.

SHIRTY. Easily offended. A man who has quickly lost his temper is said to have got his shirt out.

SHOD. [Perfect of Shed.] Spilt. This word is correct, the Anglo-Saxon past tense being sceód.

"I sent him up to fetch a little beer, but he shod half of it bringing of it home."

SHOES AND STOCKINGS, *m.* A wild flower of the *cypripedium genus* (Holloway) called in East Sussex "pattens and clogs," or "butter and eggs."

SHOG. The core of an apple.

SHOKE, *m.* The original form of shook.

"He shoke his fistes in my face, he did!"

SHOOKED, *e.* Shook.

"I shooked in my shoes to hear what words he used."

SHOOLER, *e.* An idle, lazy fellow; described as "a man who goes about with his boots undone."

SHOOT, *w.* A young growing pig. (See Sheat.)

SHOOT. A gutter round a roof for shooting off the water.

SHORE, *m.* To shelve off; to cut off evenly.

"If the road was better shored at the sides the water wouldn't lay so much as what it does."

SHORE. [*Schoren*, Dutch, to prop up.] A prop, a support.

SHORN-BUG, *m.* [*Scearn*, Ang. Sax., dung; *scearn-wibba*, a shorn-bug.] A beetle. To eat shorn-bugs for dinner is a proverbial expression for the extremity of poverty.

SHORT, *m.* Out of temper; unable to give a civil answer.

SHORT, *m.* Tender.

A rat-catcher once told me that he knew many people who were in the habit of eating barn-fed rats, and he added, "When they're in a pudding you could not tell them from a chick, they eat so short and purty."

SHOVE, *e.* To put the loose corn into cops or heaps, that it may be more conveniently taken up.

A Dictionary of the Sussex Dialect. 105

Shrape, *e.* To scold.

Shravey.* A loose sub-soil, something between clay and sand.

Shrievy, *e.* Unravelled; having threads withdrawn.

Shrogs, *e.* The refuse trimmings of hop-plants; also called chogs.

Shruck, *e.* Shocked.

Shruck, *e.* Shrieked.
> An old woman who was accidentally locked up in a church where she was slumbering in a high pew, said, "I shruck till I could shruck no longer, but no one comed, so I up and tolled upon the bell."

Shuck. Another form of the perfect tense of the verb to shake.

Shuck, *e.* To undress; to shell peas, &c.

Shuck, *m.* A husk or pod.

Shuckish. Unsettled; applied to the weather.

Shun. To push. "He shunned me off the pavement."

Shut, *w.* A young pig; also called a sheat or shoot.

Shut-of, *m.* To be rid of.
> "Once he gets indoors, you'll be troubled to get shut an' him; I dunno but what you'd best shun him out of the fore-door at oncest." (Pronounced Wunst.)

Sideboards, *w.* Rails fitted on the top of the sides of a wagon, so as to admit of the addition of an extra load.

Sidelands, *w.* The outside parts of a ploughed field, adjoining the hedges, where the plough has been turned, running parallel with the lands or warps.

Sidy.* Surly; moody.

Siever, *e.* All the fish caught at one tide.

Silt, *e.* Sand or mud deposited and left by the tide or a flood.

Silt-up. To become so choked-up, with mud or sediment of any kind, as to stop the passage of water in a ditch or the bed of a river.

Simple, *e.* Unintelligible, or stupid.
> "Will you be so good as to lend mother another book? for she says this one is so simple she can't make it out at all."

Sissel, *m.* The usual pronunciation of thistle.

Sizzing. Yeast or barm. It is probable that this word may have its origin in the sound made by beer or ale in working.

Skeeling.* The bay of a barn; the side of a garret or upper room, where the slope of the roof interferes with the upright."

Skep. [*Scep*, Ang. Sax., a basket.] A beehive, or the straw hackle placed over it for protection.

Skep, *e.* A hat; a broad flat basket.

Skice. To run quickly and slily, so as to avoid detection.
"I just saw the top of his skep as he skiced along under the hedge."

Skid. To check a wheel going down hill.

Skid-pan. The iron used for skidding.

Skim-coulter. That part of a plough which goes in front to take off the turf.

Skinny, *w.* Mean; inhospitable.

Skip, *e.* A small wooden or metal vessel for taking up yeast.

Skirmish, *m.* To run about in a mischievous manner.
"It's no use to try and keep a garden tidy as long as the children are a skirmishing about over the flower borders."

Skitterwaisen, *w.* From corner to corner. (Probably a corruption of Caterwise.)

Skivel, *w.* A skewer. In the west, dogwood, of which skewers are made, is called skiver-wood.

Skreel, *e.* To scream.

Skrow. Surly; ill-tempered.

Slab, *m.* A rough board; the outside cut of a tree which has been sawn up in planks.

Slabby, *m.* Dirty; wet and slippery; greasy; sticky.
"Make the gruel thick and slab."
—*Macbeth*, Act iv. sc. 1.

Slack, *m.* Loose conversation.

Slam. To do any work in a slovenly manner.

Slap, *m.* In good condition; hearty.
"I don't feel very slap this morning."

Slappel.* A portion; a large rough piece of anything.

Slat, *m.* A slate.

SLATES, *m.* The pods of peas, &c.

"The peas seem to be out in bloom a long time before they hang in slates this year."

SLAVVEN. A large piece. (See Slappel.)

SLAY, or SLEIGH. A slope.

SLEECH, *e.* Mud or sea-sand used as manure. The sediment deposited by the river Rother is called sleech.

SLICK. [*Slikr*, Icel., smooth.] To comb the hair; to make it sleek.

This word is used frequently in America in this sense.

SLIM. [*Slim*, Dutch. *Schlimm*, German, bad; sly.] To do work in a cunning, deceitful manner.

SLING. A cow or ewe which brings forth her young prematurely is said to sling her calf or lamb.

SLIPE. To take off the outside cover from anything; especially used of removing the bark from trees.

SLIRRUP. To lap up any liquid noisily.

SLIT.* [Connected with the Dutch word *sluiten*, to shut or lock.] To thrust back the lock of a door without the key.

SLIVER, *w.* [*Slifan*, Ang. Sax., to cleave.] A slice.

SLOCK, *e.* [Corruption of Slack.]

SLOCKSEY, *e.* Slovenly. (Probably connected with the word slack.)

SLOMMAKY, *m.* Untidy; dirty.

SLOP, *m.* [*Slóp*, Ang. Sax.] A short full-made frock, of coarse material, worn by men over their other clothes; it reaches to the waist, where it is fastened by a band.

SLUB. Thick mud; used as slush is elsewhere.

SMEECH, *m;* or SMUTCH, *e.* [*Sméc*, Ang. Sax., smoke, vapour.] A dirty black sort of smoke or mist.

In the west of England the word means a stench, and is applied to the smell of the snuff of a candle.

SMOCK-WINDMILL. A windmill boarded down to the ground, as opposed to a post-mill.

SMOLT, *e.* [*Smolt*, Ang. Sax., smooth.] Smooth and shining.

SMOORN, *e.* To smear.

SMUTCH, *e.* To smudge.

"What, hast smutched thy nose!"
—*Winter's Tale*, Act i. sc. 2.

SNAG. The common snail. With respect to this word, which I had been inclined to derive from the Anglo-Saxon *snæg-el*, Mr. Skeat informs me that it is the old original word of which *snæg-el* is the diminutive; hence snag is not derived from *snæg-el*, but *vice versa*.

The children say,—
> "Snag, snag, put out your horn,
> And I will give you a barley corn."

SNAP-PLOUGH, *w*. A plough with two wings, so fixed as to snap or move from one side to the other, though only one projects at a time.

SNETHE, *m;* or SNEAD, *w*. [*Snæd*, Ang. Sax.] The long handle of a scythe.

SNICKER, *m*. [*Snikken*, Dutch, to gasp.] To sneer; to laugh inwardly.

SNIGGLER, *m*. A slight frost.

SNOB, *m*. [Connected with Icel., *snápr*, a fool and knave.] A travelling shoemaker; a cobbler.

In the neighbourhood of Burwash it is considered a most unfavourable description of a stranger to say that he is "a broken down snob from Kent."

SNOULE, *e*. A small quantity of anything. Used in Norfolk for a short thick cut from the crusty part of a loaf or a cheese.

SNUDGE, *m*. To hold down the head; to walk with a stoop looking on the ground as if in deep thought.

SNUFFY, *m*. Angry. A common nickname for a testy person.

"Old snuffy came snudging along here just now, and wanted to borrow a few Brussels sprouts, but I lent him a brockylo once and never got it back again, so I warn't a-going to be took in a second time."

SOCK, *m*. A blow.

"I'll give that old sow-cat o' yourn a sock aside the head if I catches her in my house agin!"

SOCK-LAMB, *m*. A lamb brought up by hand.

SOCKISH, *m*. (Probably a variation of Suckish.) Requiring to be petted and nursed; said of a child.

SOCKLE, *m*. To suckle.

SODGER, *m*. A red herring; literally a soldier.

The sirloin of a jackass, stuffed with sodgers, is a Sussex man's definition of coarse, uninviting food.

SOLLY, *e.* A tottering or unstable condition.

"That cart-lodge of Mus' Dicksey's is all of a solly; t'wunt least but a very little while longer afore it comes down."

SOME-ONE-TIME, *m.* Now and then; occasionally.

"Some-one-time I goos across to the Chequers, but doänt make no rule of it."

SOMEWHEN. At some time.

SOOKLAND, *e.* A name in the manor of Wadhurst for assart-land.

SOOR, *m.* An exclamation expressive of surprise.

SOOR. [Corruption of Swore.]

"When I told him that the calves was got into the greenhouse, he jumped up and soor that dreadful that I was all of a shake."

SOPS-AND-ALE. A curious custom formerly prevalent at Eastbourne, which has fallen into disuse in the present century. The senior bachelor of the parish was elected by the inhabitants to the office of steward, and had committed to his charge a damask napkin, a great wooden bowl, twelve wooden trenchers, a dozen wooden knives and forks, two wooden candlesticks, and two wooden sugar basins.

Whenever a matron within the parish increased her family, it was the duty of this official to go to the church door on the Sunday fortnight after the interesting event, and there publicly proclaim that sops and ale would be provided that evening at a certain house agreed upon, where the following arrangements were made.

Three tables were placed in some convenient room, one of which was covered with the damask table cover and furnished with a china bowl, plates, and silver-handled knives and forks; the bowl was filled with biscuits steeped in wine and sweetened with fine sugar. The second table was also covered with a cloth and decently provided with knives, forks and china, and a bowl containing beer-sops sweetened with fine sugar. The third table had no cloth, was furnished with the wooden trenchers, candlesticks, &c., and had its wooden bowl filled with beer-sops sweetened with the coarsest sugar. After evening prayers the company assembled at the house of their entertainer, and were placed in the following order:—Those persons whose wives had presented them with twins sat at the first table, and were addressed as "benchers;" those whose partners had blessed them in a less degree were ranged round the second table; while those who were married but childless, were placed with the old bachelors at the third table. Various toasts were given, and the company always broke up at the temperate hour of eight, "generally very cheerful and good tempered."

—*Sussex Archæological Collections*, vol. xiii. p. 228.

Soss-about, *e.* To mix different things together; generally applied to liquids.

"To soss" in the North means to go about in the dirt.

Sossel. To make a slop.

Sow. A word used among the old Sussex iron-workers for a weight of 2,000-lbs.

Sow-cat, *m.* A female cat.

Sow-waps. The queen wasp.

In some parts of the county a reward of sixpence is offered for each sow-waps killed in the spring.

Space. A measurement of three feet. Spaces and rods are almost the only terms of measurement I have ever heard used by country people.

Space. To measure ground.

Spalt, *e.* [Connected with the Dutch *spalten*, to split.] Split; brittle; decayed. Applied to timber.

Spalter, *w.* To split or chip off.

Spannel, *m.* To make dirty foot marks about a floor, as a spaniel dog does.

"I goos into the kitchen and I says to my mistus, I says ('twas of a Saddaday), the old sow's hem ornary, I says. Well, says she, there aint no call for you to come spanneling about my clean kitchen any more for that, she says; so I goos out and didn't say naun, for you can't never make no sense of women-folks of a Saddaday."

Shakespeare uses the word in the sense of dogging the steps,—

"The hearts that spaniel'd me at heels."

—*Anthony and Cleopatra*, Act iv. sc. 10.

Spanner, *w.* A wrencher; a nut-screw.

Span-new. Quite new.

Spar. [*Spére*, Ang. Sax., a spear.] A stick pointed at each end, and doubled and twisted in the middle; used by thatchers to secure the straw on the roof of a stack or building.

Sparr. [Corruption of Sparrow, as Barr for Barrow.]

Spartacles. [An invariable corruption of Spectacles.]

Spat. A slap or blow.

Spats, *m.* Leather gaiters reaching above the knee.

Spattledashes, *m.* Short leather gaiters not reaching much above the ankle.

Spear, *m.* The sting of a bee.
> A bee is always said *to bite* in Sussex.

Spear. To sprout up out of the ground.
> "Soonsever the peas begins to spear, the meece and the sparrs gets holt an' em."

Spelts. Iron toes and heels for boots.

Spenes. [*Spana*, Ang. Sax.] The teats of a cow.

Spene. The prong of a pitchfork.

Spet. Spit.
> "The old cat set there, and there she set, and spet and soor and went on all the whole time."

Spice. [*Espéce*, French.] A slight attack of illness.
> "I had a spice of the ague last week, and I doànt want no more of him, for all that they says 'tis worse *not* to have him than 'tis to!'"

Spile, *w.* A spigot.

Spilt. [*Spillan*, Ang. Sax., to spoil.] Spoiled.
> "She shod the milk all over her, and spilt her new frock."

Spilwood. Refuse of wood; wood spilt (or spoilt) by the sawyers.

Spinney. A thicket; a small plantation.

Spit, *m.* As much earth as can be taken up at once with a spade.

Spit-deep, *m.* As deep as a spade goes in digging.

Splash, *m.* To bank up a hedge.

Splash, *e;* or **Splisher,** *m.* To lay a live hedge.

Spong, *e.* To cobble; to work in a rough clumsy way with a needle.

Sprackish, *w.* Smart and active.

Spray-wood. Fagots of brushwood used in the ovens.

Spread-bat, *e.* A wooden bar, used to keep the chains apart from rubbing the horses' legs and sides when drawing a plough or harrow.

SPROG.* A linch-pin.

SPRONG, *e;* or SPRONK, *m.* The roots of a tree or a tooth.

SPRONKY, *m.* Full of roots.
> "Ah! I guv' old Mus' Tweazer the biggest job o' tooth-pulling ever he had! It took him purty nigh two hours! and he said he'd never seen such a tooth all his days, to goo so fur down nor yet to be so spronky."

SPRUG, *e.* To smarten.

SPRY, *e.* Gay; cheerful.
> A word frequently used in America, meaning "in good health."

SPUD. A light garden tool with a long handle, for cutting up weeds.

SPUDDLE, *m.* To use a spud.
> "I be gettin' in years and can't do no more than just doddle about the ground and spuddle up a few weeds."

SQUAB. A young unfledged bird.

SQUACKETT, *m.* To quack like a duck.
> "I thought Mus' Reynolds was about last night, the ducks kep all on squacketting so."

SQUAT, *w.* To indent or bruise anything by letting it fall.

SQUAT-BAT, *e.* A piece of wood used for stopping a wheel while the horses are at rest on a hilly road.

SQUATTY, *w.* Said of meal that has fermented.

SQUENCH, *m.* [Corruption of Quench.]

SQUINNEY. To squint; to pry about.

SQUIRM. To wriggle like an eel.

STAB. A small hole in the ground in which the rabbit secures her young litter.

STABBLE, *e.* To make a floor dirty by walking on it in wet or muddy shoes.

STADE, *e.* [*Stede*, Ang. Sax.] A shore where ships can be beached; a landing place.

STALDER. [*Stælan*, Ang. Sax., to place.] The stool on which casks are placed in a cellar.

STALLAGE, *m.* (Same as Stalder.)

A Dictionary of the Sussex Dialect.

STALLED, *e.* Tired; satiated.

"Aint you fairly stalled of waiting?"

"I think the old dog has stalled himself now, for he found a stab out in the field and eat the lot."

STAMMERS. The fresh shoots of a tree which has been cut back.

STAM-WOOD, *m.* [*Stam*, Dutch, a stem; a trunk of a tree.] The roots of trees, stubbed or grubbed up.

STANDING. A stall at a market or fair.

STARK, *e.* [*Sterc*, Ang. Sax., rigid.] Ground is said to be stark or starked up, when the surface has dried very quickly after rain.

STARKY, *e.* Flinty.

"The land is very starky."

START. An excitement; a fuss.

"There's been a pretty start up at the forge this morning! Fighting and all manner."

When a Sussex man is at a loss for words to describe events or ideas of a somewhat discreditable nature, he gets out of the difficulty by using the phrase "all manner!" If he wishes to describe great profusion and plenty, he says "there was everything of something and something of everything, as the saying is;" but where he gets the saying from I have no idea.

STATESMAN, *m.* An estates' man; a man who owns a few acres of land and farms them himself.

The general condition of such persons is that their property is mortgaged, and with much harder work they are worse off than ordinary labourers.

STEALE. [*Stela*, Ang. Sax., a handle.] The handle of most agricultural implements.

STEAN. To pave a road with stones; to line a well or a grave with stone or brick.

The Steine, at Brighton, probably derives its name from this word.

STEAN, *m.* To mark out a field for ploughing, which is usually done by placing large stones to show the lines.

STEDDLE. [*Stathol*, Ang. Sax., a basis.] The wooden framework placed on stones or other support, on which corn stacks are built.

STEDDLE, *m.* A small side table, or a temporary arrangement of boards and trestles.

STENT, *m.* A portion of work appointed to be done in a set time.

STEW. A pool in which fish are kept for the table.

STILL. Quiet; respectable.
"He's a nice still man."

STILL-WATERS. Distilled waters.
There is generally an old woman in every village who is a notable distiller of waters, which are in great request as domestic medicine.

STILTS. Crutches.
It is rather surprising to be told that a person is such a complete cripple that he can only walk with stilts.

STINT, *e.* Shabby; undergrown.

STITHE, *w.* An anvil.
"If his occulted guilt
Do not itself unkennel in one speech,
It is a damned ghost that we have seen;
And my imaginations are as foul
As Vulcan's stithy."
—*Hamlet,* Act iii. sc. 2.

STIVED-UP, *m.* Crowded.
"We were all stived-up in one room. There was four families, one in each corner, and a single man who slep' in the middle. I put up with it as long as I could, but when the single man began to take in lodgers I couldn't stand it no longer."

STIVER-ABOUT. (The i is pronounced as in shiver.) To stagger.

STOACH, *e.* To trample ground as cattle do in wet weather.

STOACH-WAY, *e.* An expression used at Rye Harbour for the channel which runs through the sand lying between the pier-head and the deep water at low tide.

STOACHY. Dirty; muddy.

STOCKY, *m.* Strong; stout; well grown.

STOCKY, *m.* Headstrong; saucy; wilful; generally said of girls.
"Since nought so stockish, hard, and full of rage,
But music for the time doth change his nature."
—*Merchant of Venice,* Act v. sc. 1.

STODGE, *e.* Thick mud. (See Stoach.)

STODGE, *m.* A fuss.

"He's always in such a stodge; if he's got to goo anywhere's he always wants to be off two hours too soon."

STOKE. To stir the fire; hence the word stoker.

STOLT, *e.* Stout; strong; generally said of fowls.

"The chickens are quite stolt."

STOMACHY, *m.* Proud; obstinate.

STONE. A weight of eight pounds.

STOOD, *m.* Stuckfast.

An old man told me, "I've seen a wagon stood in the snow on the road from Selmeston to Alciston, and they never moved it for six weeks."

STOOL-BALL. An old Sussex game similar in many respects to cricket, played by females. It has lately been revived in East Sussex by the establishment of stool-ball clubs in many villages, which not only provide good exercise for young ladies who might otherwise become lazy, but also promote kind, social intercourse among all classes. The "elevens" go long distances to play their matches; they practice regularly, and frequently display such perfection of fielding and wicket-keeping as would put most amateur cricketers to shame. The rules are printed, and are as keenly discussed and implicitly obeyed as those of the Marylebone Club.

The game is thus alluded to in Poor Robin's Almanack for 1740,—

"Now milkmaid's pails are deckt with flowers,
And men begin to drink in bowers;
Sweet sillabubs, and lip-loved tansey,
For William is prepared by Nancy.
Whilst hob-nail Dick and simp'ring Frances
Trip it away in country dances;
At stool-ball and at barley-break,
Wherewith they harmless pastime make."

STOP, *e.* A rabbit-stab; probably so-called because the doe stops up the entrance when she leaves her young.

STORM-COCK, or SREECHER. The missel thrush.

STOT, *w.* A young bullock.

STRAND, *m.* A withered stalk of grass; one of the twists of a line.

STREALE.* [*Stræl*, Ang. Sax.] An arrow.

STREET. In Sussex a road is called a street without any reference to there being houses beside it; but I am quite unable to say why some roads should be distinguished from others by being so called. (A street originally meant a paved road, from the Latin *strata via*.)

STRIDE, *m.* A long distance.

"I doänt exactly know the name of the place he's gone to, but I know 'tis a middling stride into the sheeres."

STRIG. The foot-stalk of any fruit or flower.

STRIKE. A smooth straight piece of wood, used in measuring, to strike the loose corn which lies above the level of the rim of the bushel.

In old inventories "a bushel and strike" usually go together.

STRIKE-PLOUGH, *m.* A plough used for striking out the furrows.

STRIVES, *m.* Rivalry.

"Sometimes I think those people must dress so for strives, to see who can be smartest."

STROD. A forked branch of a tree.

STROMBOLO. (Possibly connected with the Dutch *stroom-ballen*, stream or tide-balls.)

"Pieces of black bitumen highly charged with sulphur and salt, found along the coast. Called thus at Brighton, doubtless from the Flemings settled in the town. The stones have been used for fuel, and Dr. Russell applied the steam to scrofulous tumours." —*Durrant Cooper's Sussex Glossary.*

STUB, *e.* The stem which is left standing out of the ground after a tree has been cut down.

STUB, *e.* To stub a horse is to lame him by letting him tread on stubs of underwood in a cover.

STUB, *m.* To grub up trees with their roots.

STUB, *m.* To pluck chicken clean after their feathers have been pulled off.

STUCKLING. An apple-pasty made thin in the shape of a semicircle, and baked without a dish.

STUD, *m.;* STUDY, *e.* A state of thoughtfulness.

"He seems all in a stud as he walks along."

STUMP, *w.* A stump of hay is an item frequently found in farm inventories in West Sussex. It means the remains of a round stack, most of which has been cut away.

Stupe, *e.* Stupid; dull.

An old schooldame thus described the progress of a pupil (aged 5):—"He's that stupe that he can't tell 'A's' from 'V's,' and he actually doänt know the meaning of 'Verily, verily!'"

Stusnet. A skillet; a small saucepan.

Suddent, *m.* Suddenly.

Sue, *e.* To drain land; also a drain. (See Sew.)

Suent, *e.* Pleasant; agreeable.

Sullage. [*Souiller*, French, to soil.] Any filth or dirt of the nature of a sediment.

Summer, *e.* The beam which supports the bed or body of a wagon.

Summer and Winter, *w.* To have summered and wintered a person, is to have known him at all seasons and under all circumstances, both good and bad.

Suppose, *m.* This word is used not to express conjecture, but certainty.

Surelye. There are few words more frequently used by Sussex people than this. It has no special meaning of its own, but it is added at the end of any sentence to which particular emphasis is required to be given, and numerous examples of its use will be found in illustrations of other words in this dictionary.

Sushy, *e.* [*Sèche*, French, dry.] In want of water.

"I never knowed such a dry time; we're as sush as sushy."

Sussel. A disturbance; an impertinent meddling with the affairs of other people.

Sussex-moon. A man sent on in front with a lantern fastened behind him.

Sussex-pudding. A compound of flour and water made up in an oblong shape and boiled. There is a moment, when it is first taken out of the saucepan, when it can be eaten with impunity; but it is usually eaten cold, and in that form I believe that it becomes the foundation of all the ills that Sussex spirit and flesh are heir to. It promotes a dyspeptic form of dissent which is unknown elsewhere. It aggravates every natural infirmity of temper by the promotion of chronic indigestion, and finally undermines the constitution; for the first symptom of the decay of nature which a Sussex man describes is invariably that he can't get his pudding to set.

Swad, *e.* A bushel basket, generally used in selling fish.

Swade. The leather strap of a spinning-wheel.

Swading-iron, *w.* An instrument used in a blacksmith's forge.

Swallocky, *e.* A term applied to the appearance of clouds in hot weather, before a thunderstorm.

Swank, *w.* A bog; a dell or damp hollow.

Swanky, *m.* Small beer.

Swap, *m.* To reap corn and beans.

Swap-hook, *m.* The implement used for swapping.

Swarly. Ill-tempered; usually applied to animals.

Swarve, *e.* To fill up; to choke with sediment.
"Our ditch is quite swarved up."

Swath. [Pronounced swarth.] A row of cut grass or corn as it is laid on the ground by mowers or swappers.
"And there the strawy Greeks, ripe for his edge,
Fall down before him, like the mower's swath."
—*Troilus and Cressida,* Act v. sc. 5.

Sweal. [*Swélan,* Ang. Sax., to kindle.] To burn the hair; to singe a pig.

Swelt. [*Sweltan,* Ang. Sax., to die.] Hot; faint.
"Like a swelt cat, better than it looks."

Swinge. [*Swingan,* Ang. Sax.] To flog.
"I will swinge him well when I catches him."

Swingel. That part of a flail which beats the corn out of the ear.

Swork. [Corruption of Sulk.] To be angry and surly.

Sworle. To snarl like a dog.

Swymy. [Swimmy.] Giddy; faint.
"I felt so swymy that I was obliged to get up and go out of church."

T.

Tack. A peculiar flavour; a strong, rank, nasty taste.

Tack. A path or causeway.

Tackle. Working implements; machinery of any kind.

A Dictionary of the Sussex Dialect.

TACKLE. Distasteful food or drink.
"I calls this here claret wine about the poorest tackle ever I tàasted."

TAG, *e.* A sheep of the first year.

TAIL-WHEAT, *m.* The inferior grain which is left after the corn has been winnowed.

TAKENERS, *m.* Persons taken to learn a trade; young men employed in fishing boats at Brighton.

TALK THIN. To talk in a low voice.
"He talk so thin that no-one can't scarcely hear what he says."

TALWOOD, *w.* [*Tailler*, French, to cut.] Wood cleft and cut into billets for firing.

TAN-FLAWING. Taking the bark off trees, the bark itself being called tan.
"If I can get a job of tan-flawing I shall make out very well."

TAVORT. Half a bushel. (See Tovet.)

TAWER. [*Tawian*, Ang. Sax., to prepare hides.] A fellmonger; a leather dresser.

TEAM, *w.* [*Téman*, Ang. Sax., to propagate.] A litter, or a number of young beasts of any kind.
"I have got a nice team of young pigs here."

TED, *m.* To spread hay; to shake out the new mown grass.

TEDDIOUS. Fretful; difficult to please.

TEDIOUS. Excessive; very.
"I never did see such tedious bad stuff in all my life."

TELL. [*Tellan*, Ang. Sax., to count.] To count.
"Otherwhiles I be forced to tell the ship over six and seven times before I can get 'em right."

TELLER, *m;* or TILLOW, *w.* [*Telgor*, Ang. Sax., a branch.] A young oak tree.

TEMPERSOME. Hasty-tempered.

TEMPEST. When the wind blows roughly it is said to tempest.
"It tempestes so as we're troubled to pitch the hay upon to the stack anyhows in the wurreld."

TEMPESTY, *w.* A gale of wind.

Tempory. [Corruption of Temporary.] Slight; badly finished.
"Who be I? Why I be John Carbury, that's who I be! And who be you? Why, you aint a man at all, you aint! You be naun but a poor tempory creetur run up by contract, that's what you be!"

Tenantry-acre. Mr. Durrant Cooper gives the following account of this allotment:—"The proportion between the tenantry and the statue acre is very uncertain. The tenantry land was divided first into laines, of several acres in extent, with good roads, some sixteen feet wide between them; at right angles with these were formed, at uncertain intervals, tenantry roads, of some eight feet in width, dividing the laines into furlongs. In each furlong every tenant had a right to his proportion, which was set out for him, not by fixing any superficial quantity, but by measuring along the line of the tenantry road of each furlong a certain number of feet to each paul, the number of feet being the same, whatever was the depth of the furlong; thus, if the furlong, for instance, consisted of what is called a hatchet-piece, something like three-quarters of a square, the part where the piece was two squares deep would contain double the superficial contents of the portion at the other end, where the measurement next the road would be similar but the depth only one half." —*Sussex Glossary*, p. 65.

Tend. To watch.
"He can't sing in church no more, for he goos to work rook-tending, and he comes home of nights that hoarse that you can't hardly hear him speak."

Terrible. Excessively. (Pronounced tarrible, as below).

Terrier. [*Terre*, French, land.] A survey and register of land.
Two terriers were made at Brighton in the last century; the first in 1738, the second in 1792, by Thomas Budgen.

Terrify. (Usually pronounced tarrify.) To tease; to annoy.
"These here fleas tarrifies me tarrible."

Tessy, *w.* Angry. [Probably a corruption of Testy.]

That. So.
"I was that tired I didn't know how to bear myself."

Thick-of-hearing, *e.* Slightly deaf.
"Old woman, old woman, will you go a shearing?
Speak a little louder, sir, I'm rather thick of hearing.
Old woman, old woman, shall I kiss you very sweetly?
I thank you very kindly, sir, I hear you quite completely."
—*Old Sussex Rhyme.*

THICK-MILK, *m.* Hot milk thickened by the addition of a few spoonfuls of flour and sweetened.

THILLS, *w.* [*Thil*, Ang. Sax., a plank.] The shafts of a wagon or cart.

THILL-HORSE, *w;* or THILLER. The shaft horse.

"What a beard thou hast got. Thou hast got more hair on thy chin than Dobbin my thill-horse has on his tail."
—*Merchant of Venice,* Act ii. sc. 2.

THREADDLE. To thread a needle.

"Open the gates as wide as wide,
And let King George go through with his bride.
It is so dark, we cannot see
To threaddle the tailor's needle."
—*Children's Game.*

THRO. Fro. To-and-thro is always used for to-and-fro.

"He goes to-and-thro to Lewes every Tuesday and Friday."

THROT, *m.* The throat.

THROW. [Through.] A thoroughfare; a public way. The four-throws is a point where four roads meet.

THROW. To cut down trees.

TICKLER, *e.* An iron pin used by brewers to take a bung out of a cask.

TICKLE-PLOUGH, *w.* A plough with wooden beam and handles.

TIDY, *m.* A child's pinafore.

TIFFY. Touchy; irritable.

TIGHT. Drunk.

Either Sussex beer must be very strong or Sussex heads very weak, for however drunk a man may have been he will declare that he did not take more than a pint, and all his friends will make the same assertion.

TIGHTISH. Well in health.

"I'm pretty tightish thank you" is not a very common expression, because it is not considered genteel to be in perfectly good health; and to say "How well you are looking" is by no means taken as a compliment. I suspect that the height of gentility is not reached till a person dies outright, and then of course it is only reflective, and the relations take credit for it.

TIGHT-UP. To clean; to put in order.

"To tight oneself up" is to dress or put on clean clothes.

Tilth, *m.* [*Tilth*, Ang. Sax., culture.] The condition of arable land.

"He's a man as always keeps his ground in good tilth."

Tillow, *w.* (See Teller.)

Time of Day, *m.* "To pass the time of day" is to greet a person passing on the road.

"I doänt know any more of him than just to pass the time o' day."

Timmersome, *e.* Timid.

A boy, who recently stated as a valid reason for not attending evening school that he was afraid that the pharisees would interrupt him on his way home, was excused by his mother on the ground that he was "that timmersome that he couldn't abear to go out after dark."

Tinker, *w.* To mend anything clumsily.

Tippèd, *m.* Pointed.

Tip-teerers, *w.* Mummers who go round performing a sort of short play at Christmas time. (See appendix.)

Tip-tongued. To talk tip-tongued is to talk in an affected manner.

"She talks so tip-tongued and gives herself such airs."

Tire. Flax for spinning. (Probably obsolete, but frequently found in old parochial accounts).

Tissick, *m.* A tickling, faint cough.

"Punch cures the gout, the cholic and the phthisic,
And it is agreed to be the very best of physic."
—*Old Song.*

Tiver, *w.* Red ochre used for marking sheep.

To-and-agin, *m.* Backwards and forwards.

"She doddles to-and-agin."

Token, *e.* A present.

"My lad's brought me such a nice token from Rye."

Token, *m.* An apparition.

A woman who had asked me to write to the War Office for tidings of her son, whose regiment was in India, came to me a few days afterwards to say that she was sorry she had given me so much trouble, as it was no use to make any enquiries about her son for he was dead, and she knew it because she had seen his token, which had walked across the field before her and finally disappeared over the stile.

It was useless to reason with the woman, or to attempt to comfort her by reading her the reply from the War Office that her son was well. It was not till he returned home and in his own person refuted the evidence of the token that her confidence in it was at all shaken.

Tom. Any cock bird, as a tom-turkey or a tom-parrot.

"I bought two hens and a tom off old Mis Cluckleford, but I doänt know as I shall make out much with 'em, for they doänt seem none of 'em inclined to lay."

Tom-bacca. Traveller's joy. *Clematis vitalba;* also called boys'-bacca, because the boys cut the small wood in pieces to smoke like cigars.

Tommy, *m.* Bread.

Tongues, *e.* Small soles; probably so called from their shape.

Took-to, *e.* Ashamed; vexed.

"I was quite took-to when you come in, for I hadn't had time to tight-up all day."

Top-of-the-House. A person who has lost his temper is said to be up-a-top-of-the-house.

"If you says anything to him he's up-a-top-of-the-house drackly minut."

Tore-grass, *m.* [Also spelt toar-grass.] Tare-grass. The long old grass which remains in pasture during the winter.

To-rights, *m.* Completely; perfectly.

"I had my little boy into Lewes to get his likeness taken a Saddaday, and the man took him to-rights, and you'll say so when you sees it."

Toss, *e.* The mow, or bay of a barn into which the corn is put to be thrashed.

Tot, *m.* A bush; a tuft of grass.

"There warn't any grass at all when we fust come here; naun but a passel o' gurt old tots and tussicks. You see there was one of these here new-fashioned men had had the farm, and he'd properly starved the land and the labourers, and the cattle and everything, without it was hisself."

Tot, *e.* A brood of chicken; a covey of partridges.

T'other-day. If pronounced t'otherdy, means the day before yesterday.

This expression is correct, because in Early English other invariably means second, and the day before yesterday is the second day reckoning backwards. It is remarkable that

second is the only ordinal number of French derivation; before the thirteenth century it was unknown, and other was used instead of it.
—*Archæologia Cantiana*, vol. ix. *(Pegge's Kenticisms.)*

Totty-land, *e.* [*Totian*, Ang. Sax., to elevate.] High-land, frequently on a side hill; used at Hastings.

Tovet, *e.* [Two fats; a fat, or vat, is a peck.] A measure of half-a-bushel. (See Tavort.)

To-year, *w.* This year, as to-day is this day.

Track. A pathway across a field.

Trade. Anything to carry; such as a bag, a dinner basket, tools or shop-goods.

"He's a man as has always got such a lot of trade along with him."

Trade, *e.* Household goods; lumber.

Trades. [*Treads.*] The ruts in a road.

"You will never get your carriage down that laine, for it can't take the trades," *i.e.*, it cannot run in the ruts.

Train, *m.* To boil down fat for lard.

Tramp, *e.* Gin and water.

Trape. To trail; to drag along the ground.

"Her gown trapes along the floor."

Trapes-about. To run about in an untidy, slovenly manner; to allow the dress to trail on the ground.

A Sussex maid describing to another servant how her mistress went to Court, said, "And as soon as ever they sees the Queen they lets their dress-tails trapes, because it aint manners to hold 'em up."

Traverse, or **Travase.** The place adjoining a blacksmith's shop where horses are shod.

Mr. Turner had an adventure in a traverse, which he thus records in his diary:—"1758. Sept. 27. In the morn my brother and self set out for Eastbourne. We dined on a shoulder of lamb, roasted, with onion sauce—my family at home dining on a sheep's head, lights, &c., boiled. We came home about 10 p.m., but not sober. Being very drunk, my horse took the wrong way, and ran into a travase with me and beat me off."

From this it would appear as if Mr. Turner had entertained his horse as liberally as himself!

TREFT, *w.* A trivet.

TRENCHER. [*Trancher*, French, to cut off.] A wooden plate on which to cut up meat or bread.

TRENCHERMAN, *m.* A feeder.
A good trencherman is a hearty eater.
"He's a very valiant trencherman, he hath an excellent stomach."
—*Much Ado About Nothing*, Act i. sc. 1.

TRESSLES. The dung of sheep or rabbits.

TRIG, *w.* To place anything behind a wheel to prevent a carriage from slipping back on a hill.

TRIPET, *w.* A wicket gate.

TRUCK. Rubbish; odds and ends.
"There's too much truck about the floor for the house ever to look tidy."

TRUG. [*Trog*, Ang. Sax., trough.] A strong basket made of split wood, used for gardening.

TRULL. [Corruption of Trundle.] To bowl a hoop.

TRUNDLE-BED, *w.* A low bed on small castors, trundled under another in the day time.

TRUNK, *e.* To under-drain land.

TRUSSING-BEDSTEAD, *w.* [*Truss*, Old English, to pack up.] A camp bedstead which can be packed for travelling.

TRUT. A hassock or footstool.

TUCK. A pinafore worn by children.

TUCK-APRON, *m.* A long apron which is fastened round the neck and waist.

TUCK-SHELL.* A tusk.

TUG. A carriage for conveying timber.

TUGS. Iron chains which fit into the hames and shafts.

TUMBLE-DOWN GATE, *m.* A gate on a towing-path so constructed that horses may pass over it while one end is pressed down. It recovers its position through being weighted at the opposite point.

TUNNELL, *w.* A funnel.

TURMUT, *m.* [Corruption of Turnip.]
"'Twas the worst year ever I knowed for a job of turmut-hoeing, for there warn't no turmuts for anyone to hoe."

Turn-wrist Plough. [Pronounced turn-rice, and sometimes so spelt in inventories.] A plough with a moveable mould-board, which turns up the second furrow on to the first.

Tushes, *m.* Tusks; long teeth.

> "O, be advised! thou know'st not what it is
> With javelins point a churlish swine to gore,
> Whose tushes never sheathed he whetteth still,
> Like to a mortal butcher, bent to kill."
> —*Shakespeare. Venus and Adonis.*

Tussick, *m.* A tuft of rank grass.

Tween-sticks, *w.* Sticks which are used to keep horses' heads apart when working two abreast.

Twelve-monthing. A yearling calf.

Twit. To taunt; to tease.

> "And twit with cowardice a man half-dead."
> —*Henry VI.*, Act iii. sc. 2.

Twitten, *w.* A narrow path between two walls or hedges.

Two, *e.* To be at two is to quarrel.

Twort, *e.* [For thwart, a corruption of the Ang. Sax. *thweor*, perverse; froward.] Pert and saucy.

"She's terrible twort—she wants a good setting down she do; and she'll get it too. Wait till my master comes in!"

Tye, *m.* A common; a large open field.

U.

Unaccountable. A very favourite adjective which does duty on all occasions in Sussex. A countryman will scarcely speak three sentences without dragging in this word.

A friend of mine who had been remonstrating with one of his parishioners for abusing the parish clerk beyond the bounds of neighbourly expression, received the following answer:—"You be quite right, sir; you be quite right. I'd no ought to have said what I did, but I doänt mind telling you to your head what I've said a-many times behind your back—We've got a good shepherd, I says, an axcellent shepherd, but he's got an unaccountable bad dog!"

UNBEKNOWNST. Unknown.

"All I can say is, if he comes here, it's quite unbeknownst to me."

UNDERBACK. A large open vessel in a brewhouse, which is placed under the mash-tun.

UNFORBIDDEN, *e.* [*Unforboden*, Ang. Sax., undaunted.] Daring; disobedient.

UNKED. [*Uncwyde*, Ang. Sax., solitary.] Lonely; dreary; dismal.

UNKED. Having the appearance of evil; betokening bad weather.

UNLUCKY. Always in mischief.

UP. To get up.

"Soonsever he comes in at the fore-door his missus she ups and pulls his hair."

UP-A-TOP-OF-THE-HOUSE. In a rage.

"He's so hot headed, he's up-a-top-of-the-house in a minut."

UPPISH. Pettish; out of temper; easily provoked.

UPSET. To find fault; to interfere with; to attack.

UPSTANDING. Upright; honourable.

"They're such an upstanding, downsitting family, you wont find their match, search England through."

USAGE, *w.* Provisions given to workmen besides their wages, called also 'lowance (allowance).

V.

VAIL. A present given to a servant over and above wages (like the French *pourboire*). The word is contracted from avail, and originally meant an advantage.

"Welcome shall they be;
And all the honours, that can fly from us,
Shall on them settle; you know your places well;
When better fall, for your avails they fell."

—*All's Well that Ends Well*, Act iii. sc. 1.

Valiant, *w.* [*Vaillant*, French.] Stout; well-built.

"What did you think of my friend who preached last Sunday, Master Piper?"

"Ha! he was a valiant man; he just did stand over the pulpit! Why you beànt nothing at all to him! See what a noble paunch he had!"

Vallers. Fallows. Spelt vallowes in Humphrey's inventory, 1697.

Vent, *e.* A place where several roads meet, generally pronounced went. (See Went.)

Vert. [*Vert*, French.] Green. Still retained in the names of fields, as The Lower Vert Field, at Selmeston.

Vivers. [*Viviers*, French.] Fish-ponds.

Vlick, *w.* To smooth the hair.

Vlothered, *e.* Agitated; flustered.

"I was so vlothered I did'nt know what to be at."

Voller, or Vollow, *m.* A fallow field.

Voor, *m.* A furrow. Contracted as barr for barrow.

W.

Want, *w.* An abbreviation of warrant.

"He wunt give ye naun I want ye."

Wanty, *w.* [*Wamb-tige*, Ang. Sax., a belly band.] The girth which is fastened to the thills of a cart, and, passing under the horse's belly, prevents the cart from tilting back.

Waps. [*Wæps*, Ang. Sax.] A wasp. (Pronounced Wops.)

Waps-hyme, *w.* A wasp's nest.

Wapsey, *m.* Spiteful; waspish.

"These bees of yours are terr'ble wapsey."

Warp. A piece of land consisting of ten, twelve, or more ridges, on each side of which a furrow is left to carry off the water.

WARP, *e.* Four herrings.

WASE.* A small bundle of straw.

WATER-COWEL, *w.* A large wooden tub.

WATER-TABLE. A low part on the side of a road, or a small cutting across a hill-road to carry off the water.

WATTLE. [*Watel*, Ang. Sax.] A hurdle.

WEALD. [*Weald*, Ang. Sax., a forest.]
　　The name given in Sussex to the large woodland tract of country which extends from the Downs, with which it runs parallel to the Surrey Hills. It was formerly an immense forest, called by the Britons Coit-Andred, and by the Saxons Andredes-weald.　　　　　　　　—*Durrant Cooper.*

WEAN-GATE. [*Wæn gedt*, Ang. Sax.] A wagon gate.

WEAN-HOUSE. [Pronounced Wenhus.] A wagon shed.

WEAN-YEAR-BEAST, *w.* A calf weaned during the current year.

WEEZE, *e.* [*Wæs*, Ang. Sax., water.] To ooze.

WENT, *e.* A crossway.
　　"Just as gate (from the verb go) means a street in Old English, so went (from the verb wend) means a lane or passage."　　　　　　　　—*Pegge's Alphabet of Kenticisms.*

WEST-COUNTRY-PARSON, *e.* The hake, so called from the black streak on the back, and abundance of the fish along the western coast.

WET. To wet the tea, is to make tea. To wet the bread, is to mix the water in the flour.

WHAPPLE-GATE. A gate on a whapple-way.

WHAPPLE-WAY. A bridle way through fields or woods.

WHEELS, *m.* A hand cart.
　　"I can get my wheels through the whapple-gate, and that often saves me a journey fetching wood."

WHIFFLE, *m.* To come in gusts.
　　"I see there had been just rain enough to whiffle round the spire whiles we was in church."

WHILES. Whilst. As amonges has been corrupted to amongst, so whiles is the original and correct form of whilst.

WHILK, *e.* To howl like a dog.

WHILK, *e.* To mutter to oneself.

Whist, *m.* Silent.

"Bide whist! I hears un!!"

White-herring. A fresh herring, as distinguished from a dried one, which is called a red-herring.

Whittle. [*Hwitel*, Ang. Sax., a white mantle.] A mantle of coarse stuff formerly worn by country women.

Wild. The Weald of Sussex is always spoken of as The Wild by the people who live in the Downs, who by the same rule call the inhabitants of the wealden district "the wild people."

Will-led, *e.* Led away or bewildered by false appearances, as a person would be who followed the Will o'Wisp.

Wide-of. Out of the direct road, but not far off.

"Stone is a little wide of Rye."

Widows-bench. (See Bench.)

"And that if any tenant having any land either fforrep or board die seized, his widow after his death sho'd have the said lands which were her said husbands at the time of his death by the custom of the said manor as by her bench dureing her natural life, altho she marry afterward to another husband." —*Bosham Manor Customs.*

Wim. To winnow corn.

Windrow, *m.* Sheaves of corn set up in a row one against the other; a thin row of new mown grass raked up lightly so as to allow the wind to pass freely through it and dry it.

Windrow. To put hay into windrows.

Windshaken, *e.* Thin; puny; weak.

"He's a poor windshaken creetur."

Wint, *e.* [*Windan*, Ang. Sax., to turn.] Two ridges of ground which are ploughed by going to one end of the field and back again. Arable land which is harrowed twice over is said to be harrowed a wint (or a turn); if three times, a wint and a half.

Winnowing-fag, *w.* A rough machine for winnowing.

Winterpicks. Blackthorn berries.

Winter-proud. Cold.

"When you sees so many of these here winterpicks about, you may be pretty sure t'will be middlin' winter-proud."

A Dictionary of the Sussex Dialect.

WIPPANCE, *w.* The bar on which the traces of a horse are hooked, and by which he draws his load. Also called whippel tree, or whipple tree.

WIPPEN. Same as wippance.

WISH. [*Wesc*, Ang. Sax., a washing.] A damp meadow; a marsh, or low land in a nook formed by the bend of a river or stream, and liable to be flooded.

WITHY. The willow. *Salix*, various species.

WRATCH, or RATCH, *e.* [*Hroécan*, Ang. Sax., to reach; extend to.] To stretch.

WRIST, or RISE. The moveable wing of a turn-wrist plough.

WROCKLED, *e.* Wrinkled.

WUTS. [Corruption of Oats.]

Y.

YAFFLE, *e.* The green woodpecker.

YANGER, *e.* [Corruption of Yonder.]
"I see an old yaffle in de 'ood yanger."

YAPE, *e.* To gossip.

YAR. Aghast; frightened.

YARBS, *w.* Herbs.

An old man in East Sussex said that many people set much store by the doctors, but for his part, he was one for the yarbs, and Paul Podgam was what he went by. It was not for some time that it was discovered that by Paul Podgam he meant the polypodium fern.

YEASTY, *m.* [Ang. Sax., *yst*, a storm.] Gusty; stormy.
"A little rain would do us good, but we doänt want it too oudacious yeasty."

"Though the yesty waves
Confound and swallow navigation up."
—*Macbeth*, Act iv. sc. 1.

YAT, *m.* A gate.

Yeild-it, *e.* Give up.

A farmer took his team to harrow a piece of wheat, but finding it too wet he said to his carter "Come along home, we'll yeild it."

Yetner. [*Git nd*, Ang. Sax., not as yet.] Not nearly. The reduplication of the negative is very common in Sussex.

"I bëant farty year old yetner."

Yoe, *m.* [Corruption of Ewe.] From the Ang. Sax., *eowu*.

Yoyster, *m.* To play about roughly and noisily.

ADDENDA.

While my Dictionary was in the press, I received the following words from the Rev. A. F. Kirkpatrick, Trinity College, Cambridge, and Edgar Sharpe, Esq., Carshalton. They came too late to be placed in their alphabetical order, but were too interesting to be omitted.

ABILITY. A word occuring in old account books for an assessment rate, now probably obsolete.

ASH-CLOTH, *m.* Before the use of soda was understood, the washerwomen used to soften the water by straining it through a coarse cloth, which was fastened over the top of the wash tub and first covered with marsh-mallow leaves, and then with a layer of wood ashes.

BAIL, *w.* The handle of a bucket, pail or kettle.

BATS. Logs of wood for burning.

BILLUS, *w.* To beat; to flog.

BLACK-GRASS, *e.* *Alopecurus agrestis.*

BLOBTONGUE, *w.* [*Blabbre*, Danish, to gabble.] A tell-tale. (See Blobtit.)

BLUE-BOTTLE, *m.* The wild hyacinth. *Hyacinthus non scriptus.*

BODGE, *w.* A water cask on wheels. (See Budge.)

BOND. [*Bond*, Ang. Sax.] A band, as a hay-bond, bonds for fastening up the sheaves of corn, &c.

BOOK. A word used in old parochial accounts for a rate, as "a 2s. 6d. book produces £500 in Horsted Keynes."

BREAK. A cultivator used among potatoes and hops. (See Idget.)

BROKE, *w.* A large quantity of timber.

Bullock-leaze. The right of turning one bullock out on a common to graze. (Used at Berwick and other places.)

Bury. A rabbit hole; a hole made by any animal.

Caffincher, *w.* The chaffinch.

Cardious. A mixed cloth made of wool and linen thread. A word which frequently occurred in old account books when spinning-wheels were in use.

Carriers. Part of a spinning-wheel fitted with wire hooks through which the thread passed to the reel.

Cast. The second swarm from a hive of bees.

Caulker-bridge, *w.* A rough bridge made of logs and fagots.

Chip, *w.* The wooden part of a plough to which the share is fastened.

Chipper, *w.* Lively; cheerful.

Church-steeple, *w.* The common agrimony. *Agrimonia rupatoria.*

Cove. A lean-to, or low building with a shelving roof. Pigeon-cotes are frequently called pigeon-coves in East Sussex.

Curmudgeon, *w.* To mend up old clothes. A curmudgeon originally meant a hard-bargainer, a miserly fellow, and probably this meaning of the word is connected with mending up rags in a miserly manner.

Cuts, *w.* The cross-beams on the floor of a wagon.

Dogger, *w.* A support for the shafts of a cart.

Ears. The irons to which the bail of a bucket is fastened.

Grandmother's-nightcap. The white campion. *L. dioica.*

Hatchet-pieces. Paul-pieces of land of irregular shape. (See Tenantry-acre.)

Hempshare, or Hemshare. Certain lands in the centre of Brighton, so named from having been used by persons engaged in the fishing trade for growing hemp for rope-making. The word is found in the court rolls, 1660.

Herring-hang, *e.* A place where herrings are hung up to dry; also called a dee.

Leakway. A road dividing one furlong from another in the tenantry-acre. (See Tenantry-acre.)

Lily, *m.* The field convolvulus. *Convolvulus arvensis.*

Merry-tree, *w.* The wild cherry tree.

Milk-maids, *w.* Birds-foot trefoil. *Lotus corniculatus.*

Sheep-leaze. The right of turning out one sheep to feed on a common.

The following words (kindly sent to me by Frederick E. Sawyer, Esq., of Brighton), are from the Brighton "Costumal," 1580; *i.e.*, a book of certain customs, chiefly relating to fishing, which received Royal confirmation at that date:—

Cocks. [*Kog, Kogge,* Danish.] Small boats, from two to six tons burden, used in the herring fishery. Their period of fishing was called cock-fare, and their nets cock-heaks.

Fare. [An old English word, probably connected with the German *fahren*, and Dutch *vaer*.] A period during which certain kinds of fishing took place; as shotnet-fare, tuck-net-fare, cock-fare, &c.

Flew. [*Flouw, Vlouw,* Dutch.] A kind of fishing-net. (A flew-net, on land, is a net hung on poles for catching woodcocks.)

Flewers. Boats of eight to twenty tons burden, used in herring fishery. (Probably boats used with the flew-nets.)

Heak. Another name for the flew.

Erredge (History of Brighton) says that in Yorkshire the nets used for fishing in the river Ouse are still called heaks.

Mox. [Ang. Sax., *max;* Dutch, *masche.*] The mesh of a net. (Called at Hastings a moak.)

Norward. A peculiar kind of net.

Rann. A division of a net. Nets are ordered to be "in deepness two ranns, every rann fifty moxes deep."

Shotters. Boats of six to twenty-six ton burden, used in the mackerel fishery.

Tacheners. Young men employed in the fishing boats. (Possibly so called from being *taken* to learn the trade.)

Tuckers. Small boats of about three tons burden, used in fishing for plaice.

APPENDIX.

THE MUMMERS' PLAY.

Dramatis Personæ.

FATHER CHRISTMAS.	A TURKISH KNIGHT.
ST. GEORGE.	A DOCTOR.

Father Christmas.—Here come I, Old Father Christmas.
  Christmas or not,
  I hope Old Father Christmas
  Will never be forgot.

  Make room, make room here, gallant boys,
   And give us room to rhyme;
  We're come to show activity,
   Upon a Christmas time.
  Acting youth or acting age,
  The like was never acted on this stage;
  If you don't believe what I now say,
  Enter, St. George, and clear the way!

St. George.—Here come I, St. George the valiant man,
  With naked sword and spear in hand;
  Who fought the dragon and brought him to the slaughter,
  And for this won the King of Egypt's daughter.
  What man or mortal dare to stand
  Before me with my sword in hand?
  I'll slay him and cut him as small as the flies,
  And send him to Jamaica to make mince-pies.

Turkish Knight.—Here come I, a Turkish Knight,
  In Turkish land I learned to fight;
  I'll fight St. George with courage bold,
  And if his blood's hot will make it cold.

St. George.—If thou art a Turkish Knight
Draw thy sword, and let us fight.

They fight; the Turk is killed.

St. George.—Ladies and gentlemen,
You see what I've done,
I've cut this Turk down,
Like the evening sun.
Is there any doctor that can be found,
To cure this Knight of his deadly wound?

Doctor.—Here come I, a doctor,
A ten pound doctor;
I've a little bottle in my pocket
Called hokum, shokum, alicampane.
I'll touch his nose, eyes, mouth and chin,
And say, "Rise, dead man," and he'll fight again.

The Turk, having been carefully examined by the doctor, is restored, and immediately indicates his readiness to renew the combat.

St. George.—Here am I, St. George, with shining armour bright,
I am a famous champion, also a worthy Knight.
Seven long years in a close cave was kept,
And out of that into a prison leaped;
From out of that into a rock of stones,
There I laid down my weary bones.
Many a giant did I subdue,
And ran a fiery dragon through.
I fought the man of Tillowtree,
And still may gain the victory.
First I fought in France,
Then I fought in Spain,
And now I've come to Selmeston
To fight the Turk again.

They fight again, and St. George is again the conqueror.

St. George.—Where is the doctor that can be found,
To cure the Turk of his deadly wound?

Doctor.—Hocus, pocus, alicampane,
Rise Turkish Knight to fight again.

Ladies and gentlemen, our play is ended,
Our money-box is recommended;
Copper or silver or gold if you can,
Five or six shillings will do us no harm.

At Salisbury the Mummers used to be called John Jacks, and there was a fifth performer called John Jack, who was represented with a large hump-back, and concluded the play by coming forward and saying,—

> Here come I,
> Little John Jack,
> With my wife and family at my back,
> Roast beef, plum-pudding, and mince-pie,
> No one loves them better than I!
>
> God save the Queen!

ANGLO-SAXON NAMES

IN SUSSEX.

The following Anglo-Saxon words will be traced in the names of almost all the towns and villages in Sussex:—

BECC. A brook. *Beck.* Bexhill.

BÚR. A cottage; a dwelling. Edburton.

BURH. A hill; a citadel. Burghersh; Bury; Pulborough.

BURNE. A stream; a river. *Bourne.* Eastbourne.

CEASTER. A camp. (From Lat. *castrum.*) *Chester.* Chichester.

COMB. A valley. (From Welsh *cwm.*) *Combe.* Balcombe.

COTE. A cot. Woodmancote; Coates.

CROFT. A small enclosed field. Wivelscroft.

DAL. A valley. *Dell; del.* Arundel.

DENU. A valley. *Den; dean.* Marden; Westdean.

DÚN. A hill; a down. *Don.* Slindon.

EA. Water; marshy place. *Ea.* Selsea; Winchelsea.

FELD. An open field; pasture; plain. *Field.* Heathfield.

FOLDE. A field. *Fold.* Slinfold.

GAT. A gate; or rather, a way; street. *Gate.* Rogate; Eastergate.

Græf. A grave; or a grove. *Grove.* Boxgrove.

Ham. A village; an enclosed place. *Ham.* Beddingham.

Hou. A hill. *Hoe.* Piddinghoe; Houghton.

Holt. A grove. Wigginholt.

Hurst. A wood. Nuthurst.

Ig. An island. *Ey.* Thorney.

Ing. A meadow. Angmering.

Ing. Used as a patronymic; thus Wilming would signify the descendants of Wilm; whence Wilmington; Rustington, &c.

Leag. A pasture. *Ley.* Earnley.

Mere. A pool or lake. *Mare; mere.* Haremare; Tangmere.

Mersc. A marsh. *Marsh.* Peasmarsh.

Stede. A place; a station. *Stead; sted.* Eastgrinstead; Horsted.

Stóc. A place. *Stock; stoke.* West Stoke.

Tún. A close; a field; a dwelling. *Ton.* Alciston.

Weorthig. A farm; an estate; a public way. *Worth.* Fittleworth.

Wic. A dwelling place; a village. *Wick.* Wick; Terwick.

Wincel. A corner. Winchelsea. (See *Wincel* in Bosworth, who gives this example.)

SUSSEX SURNAMES.

The following names of families, now residing in the county, are derived from or connected with Sussex words which will be found in this dictionary:—

AKEHURST. [Ang. Sax., *āc*, an oak, and *hurst*, a wood.]

ASHBURNHAM. [Ang. Sax., *æsc*, an ash; *burne*, a stream, and *hám*, a dwelling.

ASHDOWN. *Æsc*, an ash, and *dún*, a hill.

ASHENDEN. *Æsc*, an ash, and *denu*, a valley.

BALKHAM. *Balca*, a ridge, and *hám*, a dwelling.

BARTON. *Barton*, a farm-yard. [Ang. Sax., *bere-tún*, an enclosure.]

BECK. *Beck*, a brook. [Ang. Sax., *becc*.]

BENTLEY. *Bent*, a tuft of grass, and *ley* (Ang. Sax., *leag*), a pasture.

BICKLEY. *Beck*, a brook, and *ley*, a pasture.

BINSTEAD. *Bin* and *steddle*, a stand.

BOURNE. A stream. [Ang. Sax., *burne*.]

BOSTEL. A hill path. (See Borstal.)

BRACKFIELD. *Brake*, a fern, and *field*.

BROAD. A common.

BROOKSHAW. *Brook*, a water-meadow, and *shaw*, a wood.

BURTENSHAW. *Barton* (*bere-tún*), a homestead, and *shaw*, a wood.

BUTTERWICK. *Butter*, and *wick*, marsh-land.

BYTHAM. (By the ham). *Hám*, a dwelling.

CALLOW. [*Calo*, Ang. Sax., bald.] Smooth.

COCKINGE. *Ing* (Ang. Sax.), a son.

COMBER. *Coombe*, or *Combe* (Ang. Sax.), a valley in the downs.

COMPER. *Comp* (Ang. Sax.), a valley.

COPLEY. *Cop*, a ridge, and *ley*, a meadow.

CROCKER. *Crock* (*crocca*, Ang. Sax.), an earthen vessel.

CROFT. *Croft* (Ang. Sax.), a piece of pasture land near a house.

CROWHURST. *Crow*, and *hurst*, a wood.

DYKE. *Dike* (Ang. Sax., *dic*), a ditch.

ETHERIDGE. *Ether* (Ang. Sax., *éther*), a pliant rod, and *hedge*.

FELDWICK. *Feld*, or *field*, and *wick*, a town.

FELSTEAD. *Feld*, or *field*, and *stead*, a place.

GILHAM. *Gill*, a rivulet, and *ham*, a dwelling.

GRIST. *Grist*, a grinding; a week's allowance of flour for a family.

HASLEHURST. *Hasel*, and *hurst*, a wood.

HATCH. A gate. In North of England, a *heck*.

HAYLEY. *Hay*, and *ley*, a meadow.

HAYWARD. A hedge-warden; an officer of the lord of the manor.

HEADLAND. A part of a field.

HEATHCOTE. *Heath*, and *cote*, or *cot*, a cottage.

HENTY. *Hen*, and *tye*, a common.

HIDE. [*Hyd*, Ang. Sax.] As much land as could be tilled with one plough.

HOCKHAM. [*Hóh*, Ang. Sax., a heel, and *hám*, a meadow.]

HOCKLEY. [*Hóh* and *leag*, Ang. Sax.] Both these words mean a field of a certain shape. (See Hocklands.)

HOLT. [*Holt*, Ang. Sax., a grove.] A small plantation.

HOLTHOUSE. *Holt* and *house*.

HOOKER. } (See Hockham.)
HOOKHAM. }

HUCKWELL. *Huck*, to knock, or to spread anything about.

HURST. A wood.

HYDE. (See Hide.)

INGS. [*Ing*, Ang. Sax.] A common pasture.

KELK. *Kilk*, or charlock.

KITTLE. *Kiddle*, delicate; ticklish.

LADE. Part of a wagon.

LANGLEY. *Long* and *ley*, a meadow.

LANGRIDGE. *Long* and *ridge*.

LANGSHAW. *Long* and *shaw*, a wood.

LANGTON. *Long* and *ton*, an enclosed place.

LEE. } *Leag*, a meadow.
LEIGH. }

LINGHAM. *Ling*, a heath, and *ham*, an enclosure.

LONGBOTTOM. *Long*, and *bottom*, a valley in the downs (the long valley).

LONGHURST. The long wood.

LONGLEY. The long meadow. (See Langley.)

MEERES. *Mere*, a marsh.

NAPPER. *Napery*, linen.

PEART. Lively.

PECK. An agricultural implement.

PELLING. *Pell*, a pool, and *ing*, a pasture.

RAVENSCROFT. *Raven*, and *croft*, a field.

REEVE. An officer of the manor.

SHAW. A wood.

STEAD. An enclosed place.

SOUTHERDEN. The south valley.

WENHAM. *Wen*, or *wain*, a wagon, and *ham*, an enclosure. The wagon-house.

WENMAN. The wagon-man.

WHEATCROFT. The wheat field.

WOODWARD. An officer of the manor; a wood-warden.

WYNDHAM. *Wynd*, a path up a hill, and *ham*.

SUSSEX SURNAMES.

BOURNE. [*Burne*, Ang. Sax.] A stream.

    Boorne
    Bourne
    Bourner
    Michelbourne.

BROOK. A stream; a water-meadow.

    Brook
    Brooks
    Brookfield
    Brookshaw
    Colbrook
    Westbrook.

COMP. A valley.

    Comper
    Compton.

COOMBE, or COMBE. A hollow in the downs.

    Combe
    Comber
    Anscombe
    Balcombe
    Dunscombe
    Ellcome
    Farncomb
    Farncombe
    Lipscombe
    Titcombe
    Whitcombe
    Witcomb.

CROFT. [Ang. Sax.] A small enclosed field near a house.

    Croft
    Crofts
    Horsecroft
    Longcroft
    Pycroft
    Ravenscroft
    Tredcroft
    Wheatcroft.

Den, or Dene. A valley.

- Barnden
- Blagden
- Blunden
- Brigden
- Cobden
- Cruttenden
- Farenden
- Fogden
- Gosden
- Hebden
- Hepden
- Hobden
- Holden
- Norden
- Ockenden
- Pagden
- Pattenden
- Ramsden
- Rigden
- Standen
- Southerden
- Wickenden
- Wisden
- Witherden.

Ham. (1) A hamlet; (2) an enclosed place.

- Balkham
- Barham
- Bellingham
- Benham
- Bromham
- Clapham
- Cobham
- Coldham
- Cosham
- Gilham
- Grabham
- Gresham
- Grinham
- Hardham
- Higham
- Hockham
- Hookham
- Kingham
- Langham
- Lingham
- Lulham
- Markham
- Mepham
- Milham
- Needham
- Oldham
- Oxenham
- Packham
- Pelham
- Sandham
- Stoneham
- Stonham
- Stopham
- Southam
- Tatham
- Wenham
- Whapham
- Wickham
- Witham
- Woodham
- Woodhams
- Wyndham.

Sussex Surnames.

HURST. [Ang. Sax.] A wood.

- Hurst
- Brinkhurst
- Broadhurst
- Crowhurst
- Folkhurst
- Haslehurst
- Longhurst
- Luckhurst
- Medhurst
- Pankhurst
- Staplehurst
- Songhurst
- Ticehurst
- Wilmshurst.

LEY. [Ang. Sax., *leag.*] A pasture land.

- Ley
- Bayley
- Bentley
- Bletchley
- Burley
- Cawley
- Copley
- Cowley
- Crutchley
- Ernley
- Graveley
- Handley
- Hawley
- Hayley
- Helmsley
- Hemsley
- Henley
- Hickley
- Worsley
- Hoadley
- Hockley
- Huntley
- Langley
- Lee
- Leigh
- Longley
- Lutley
- Medley
- Morley
- Notley
- Nutley
- Oakley
- Pelley
- Rapley
- Ripley
- Stapley
- Wheatley.

SHAW. A small wood on a hill side.

- Shaw
- Bagshaw
- Brookshaw
- Burstenshaw
- Burtenshaw
- Buttonshaw
- Crawshaw
- Henshaw
- Langshaw
- Oldershaw.

STEAD. [Ang. Sax.] A place.

    Stead
    Felstead
    Grinstead
    Halstead
    Halsted
    Hempsted
    Isted
    Maxted
    Polsted
    Steadman.

WICK. [Ang. Sax.] A town.

    Wicks
    Butterwick
    Chadwick
    Feldwick
    Gratwick
    Hardwick
    Madgwick
    Markwick
    Padwick
    Rudwick
    Strudwick
    Wickerson
    Wickham
    Wickenden.

ADVERTISEMENTS.

English Dialect Society.

Director and Hon. Sec.: Rev. W. W. SKEAT, 1, Cintra Terrace, Cambridge.

Treasurer: Rev. J. W. CARTMELL, Christ's College, Cambridge.

Bankers: J. MORTLOCK & CO., Cambridge.

(London Agents: Messrs. SMITH, PAYNE & SMITH, 1, Lombard Street, E.C.)

Objects of the Society:—(1) To bring together those who are interested in the study of Provincial English; (2) to provide a common centre to which communications may be sent, with a view to gathering materials for a complete record of all Provincial English words; (3) to publish (subject to proper revision) new collections of Provincial words, as well as to reprint scarce and valuable works upon the subject; (4) to supply information to such Members as desire to help in the work.

The Subscription is *Half*-a-Guinea only per Annum, due in advance, in each year, on the 1st of January, and payable to the Treasurer, as above. The Series of Publications began in 1873; new Members can join the Society at any time and for any period. Every Member who has paid his Subscription for any year will be entitled to a copy of every publication for that year.

Members wishing to join the Society should send name and address to the Secretary, and the subscription to the Treasurer.

The Publications are all of a uniform size, viz., demy 8vo.; the Publishers are Messrs. Trübner & Co., 57, Ludgate Hill, E.C., to whom all complaints concerning non-delivery of the publications should be addressed.

Publications for 1873:—1. Seven Reprinted Glossaries, numbered B. 1 to B. 7. 2. Series A, Part 1, Bibliographical List of some Books relating to English Dialects. 3. A Glossary of Swaledale Words, by Captain J. Harland.

Publications for 1874:—4. A History of English Sounds, by H. Sweet, Esq. 5. Seven Reprinted Glossaries, numbered B. 8 to B. 14. 6. A Reprint of Ray's Glossary, ed. 1691, with additions and notes.

N.B.—Subscribers for 1874 also receive a copy of the Sussex Glossary, by the Rev. W. D. Parish.

Prospectuses can be obtained on application to the Secretary.

BIBLIOTHECA SUSSEXIANA.

A FEW BOOKS RELATING TO THE

COUNTY OF SUSSEX,

ETC., ETC., ON SALE BY

W. J. SMITH,

41, 42, 43, NORTH STREET, BRIGHTON.

Books and Prints relating to the County BOUGHT or EXCHANGED.

Volumes of the Sussex Archæological Collections always on Sale, and good prices given for any of the First Five Volumes.

Libraries and Parcels of Books Bought.

THE ARCHITECTURAL HISTORY OF CHICHESTER CATHEDRAL, with an introductory essay on the Fall of the Tower and Spire, by the Rev. R. Willis, M.A., F.R.S., &c., &c., Jacksonian Professor in the University of Cambridge; the History of Boxgrove Priory, by the Rev. J. L. Petit, M.A., F.S.A., and of Shoreham Collegiate School, together with the Collective Architectural History of the foregoing Buildings, as indicated by their Mouldings, by Edmund Sharpe, M.A., F.R.I.B.A. Illustrated by more than 100 plates, diagrams, plans and woodcuts, in royal 4to. cl. gt. top, price 15s.

A RAMBLE ON THE COAST OF SUSSEX IN 1782, by Antony Highmore, the Author of the "History of the Honourable Artillery Company," &c.—The MS. of this interesting little brochure only came to light a few weeks ago. Mr. Hindley, the Editor, has taken pains to illustrate it with Notes. It is well-printed and illustrated, 8vo. 3s. It should be in the possession of all the Members of the Sussex Archæological Society, as also of others interested in Local History. A few copies are printed on large paper, 4to., 5s.

THE CHURCHES OF SUSSEX, drawn and etched by R. H. Nibbs. Architectural and Historical descriptions are added to the plates, from the pen of M. A. Lower, Esq., F.S.A., late editor of the "Sussex Archæological Collections." The book contains 88 plates, and makes a handsome 4to. volume, in appropriate binding, for 25s., the original price being £3. 3s. The name of the artist is sufficient guarantee for the style and character of the illustrations.

MARTIN'S (P. J.) GEOLOGICAL MEMOIR ON A PART OF WESTERN SUSSEX, tables, &c., 4to. bds., 8s. 6d. (pub. 20s.) 1828.

THE WORTHIES OF SUSSEX.—Original Biographies of the celebrated Natives or Inhabitants of the County, from the earliest period to the present time, with much curious information, illustrative of Sussex History and Antiquities, by Mark Antony Lower, F.S.A., &c.; in one large royal 4to. volume, with extra plates inserted, appropriate binding, 30s. Only a few copies left.

SUSSEX HISTORY AND ANTIQUITIES.—The New History of the County of Sussex, by M. A. Lower, Esq., M.A., F.S.A. Two handsome volumes for 12s. 6d., instead of 25s.

STEMMATA SHIRLEIANA, OR THE ANNALS OF THE SHIRLEY FAMILY, 2nd edition, with numerous vignettes and many hundred engravings of arms, seals, statues, &c., and Genealogical tables, including Memorials of the Shirleys of Wiston, West Grinstead, Preston, Chiddingly, Ote Hall, Isfield, &c., and containing many interesting facts relative to the Archæology, &c., of these Sussex Parishes, demy 4to. cl., as new, £3. 3s.

THE NOTORIOUS CHICHESTER SMUGGLERS.—A full and genuine History of the Inhuman and Unparalleled Murders of Mr. William Galley, a Custom-house Officer, and Mr. Daniel Chater, a Shoemaker, by Fourteen Notorious Smugglers, with the Trials and Execution of Seven of the Bloody Criminals at Chichester. Illustrated with Seven Plates, descriptive of the Barbarous Cruelties. To which is now added an Article from the "Sussex Archæological Collections," by W. D. Cooper, Esq., on "Smuggling in Sussex." Neatly half-bound, gilt top, for 2s. 6d., or by post 2s. 9d.

BIBLIOTHECA SUSSEXIANA.

WEST TARRING AND THE NEIGHBOURHOOD OF WORTHING.—Parochial Fragments, relating to West Tarring and the Chapelries of Heene and Durrington, with Life of Thomas A'Becket, an account of his palace, and of the figs he introduced at West Tarring, and particulars relating to the learned John Selden and his cottage at Salvington, with description of Broadwater, Offington, Cissbury, Chankbury (the Sites of famous Camps), Findon, &c., by the Rev. John Wood Warter, 8vo. cl., 4s. 6d. (pub. at 10s. 6d.)

HORSFIELD'S HISTORY OF THE COUNTY OF SUSSEX, plates, 2 vols., royal 4to. hf. mor., scarce, £3. 3s.

HORSFIELD'S HISTORY AND ANTIQUITIES OF LEWES AND ITS VICINITY, with numerous extra plates inserted, containing also the Natural History of the District, by Dr. Mantell, 2 vols. sm. 4to. hf. mor., £2. 5s. 1824.

MANTELL'S FOSSILS OF THE SOUTH DOWNS, and of Tilgate Forest, or Illustrations of the Geology of Sussex, plans, sections and 52 large plates, comprising many hundred fossils, engraved by Mantell, 2 vols., 4to. bds., £3. 6s., scarce (pub. £5. 18s., 1822.) Fossils of the South Downs, 4to. bds. 35s. (pub. at £3. 3s.)

ILLUSTRATIONS OF CHURCH ARCHITECTURE IN THE COUNTY OF SUSSEX, by a local Artist, forming a supplement to Nibbs' Churches. LIST OF PLATES: CHURCHES—Amberley, Angmering and Shipley, East Lavant, Fairlight (Old) and Hardham Priory, Fletching, Hardham and Turwick, Hollington and East Marden, Houghton, Hove (Old), Lindfield, Lullington, Middleton and Clapham, Pagham, Pevensey, Rudgwick, Sidlesham, Uckfield and Durrington, West Dean, Wiggonholt, Shermanbury, Westmeston. DOORWAYS—Bramber, Shoreham (Old), Shoreham (New), Stopham and Hunston. PORCHES—Waldron and Rustington. FONTS—Burwash, Pycombe, Worth, Iford, Eartham, St. Anne's (Lewes), Shoreham (New), Buxted, Poynings, St. Nicholas (Brighton), Isfield, Clymping, Amberley and Yapton. CAPITALS—Seaford, Hurstmonceux. EFFIGIES—Ifield, Clayton, Sullington, Horsham. WINDOWS—Racton, Waldron, Alfriston, Poynings, Lewes Gateway, The Lanes (Brighton). 61 plates, on stout crayon paper, sm. fol. and enclosed in a neat portfolio, 21s.

MANTELL'S (G.) NARRATIVE OF THE VISIT OF WILLIAM IV. AND QUEEN ADELAIDE TO LEWES, October 22nd, 1830, 8vo. bds., 2s. (pub. 4s.) 1831.

MANTELL'S DAY'S RAMBLE IN AND ABOUT LEWES, vigs., plates of Antiquities, &c., 12mo. cl., 1s. 6d. (pub. 5s.) 1846.

AMSINCK'S (P.) TUNBRIDGE WELLS and its Neighbourhood, including Eridge Castle, Mayfield, Bayham, Scotney, South Park, Buckhurst, Kidbrooke, Brambletye and other places in the county of Sussex, illustrated by 43 plates, fine impressions, with a coloured plate of Tunbridge Wells, and three pencil drawings of "The High Rocks," "The Castle," and "A View near Tunbridge Wells," inserted, demy 4to. hf. bd. gilt leaves, 23s. (pub. £3. 13s. 6d.)

BOYNE'S (W.) TOKENS USED IN THE XVII. CENTURY IN ENGLAND (including Sussex), Wales and Ireland, by Corporations, Merchants, Tradesmen, &c., 42 sheets of plates containing several hundred coins, th. 8vo. cl., 8s. 6d. (pub. at £1. 11s. 6d.) 1838.

WISE (J. R.) THE HISTORY AND SCENERY OF THE NEW FOREST, Hampshire, with glossary of Provincialism, list of the flowering plants, birds, lepidoptera, &c., and a general description of the geology, botany, ornithology, archæology, &c., of the district, followed by a copious index, fine maps, plans, sections and numerous splendid illustrations by W. Crane, engraved by Linton, 8vo., green cl. gt. elegant, as new, 7s. 1867.

SUSSEX ARCHÆOLOGICAL COLLECTIONS (complete set), illustrating the History and Antiquities of the County, published by the Archæological Society, numerous engravings (some coloured), 25 vols. 8vo. cl. very scarce, £14. 14s.

Catalogue of Old Books for One Stamp.

LIBRARIES AND WASTE PAPER BOUGHT.

W. J. SMITH, NORTH ST., BRIGHTON.

In the Press, royal 4to, for early publication.

Price, 15s.; Half Morocco, 21s.

Nooks and Corners of Old Sussex.

Profusely Illustrated with Woodcuts and Plates.

It will be carefully printed on toned Paper and elegantly bound, and will contain nearly 100 pages of illustrations of all the principal objects of interest in Sussex, with brief descriptive letter-press opposite each page of engravings, and thus, in the shape of an Album, form a valuable and concise epitome of Sussex Antiquities.

As only a limited number of Copies will be printed, Subscribers are invited to make early application.

All Communications to be sent to the Editor, Rev. P. DE PUTRON, Rodmell, or to the Secretaries of the Lewes School of Science and Art, for the benefit of which Institution the work is published.

Now Ready, with Plan and more than 70 Illustrations, a new edition of

The Handbook for East Bourne,

SEAFORD, PEVENSEY CASTLE, HERSTMONCEUX CASTLE,
WILMINGTON PRIORY, MICHELHAM PRIORY,
BEACHY HEAD, HAILSHAM, &c.

BRIGHTON, LEWES, NEWHAVEN, HASTINGS, ST. LEONARDS, BATTLE, &C.

By GEORGE F. CHAMBERS, F.R.A.S.

OF THE INNER TEMPLE, BARRISTER AT LAW.

This Work contains Information greater in amount, and more varied and practical in character, than all the other Local Guide Books put together.

Sold at EASTBOURNE by nearly all the Booksellers, Stationers, &c.
London: E. STANFORD, Charing Cross.

JUST PUBLISHED.
NEW AND ELEGANT EDITIONS.
Price 6d. Each. Post Free.

TOM CLADPOLE'S
𝔍𝔲𝔯𝔫𝔢𝔶 𝔱𝔬 𝔏𝔲𝔫𝔫𝔲𝔫,

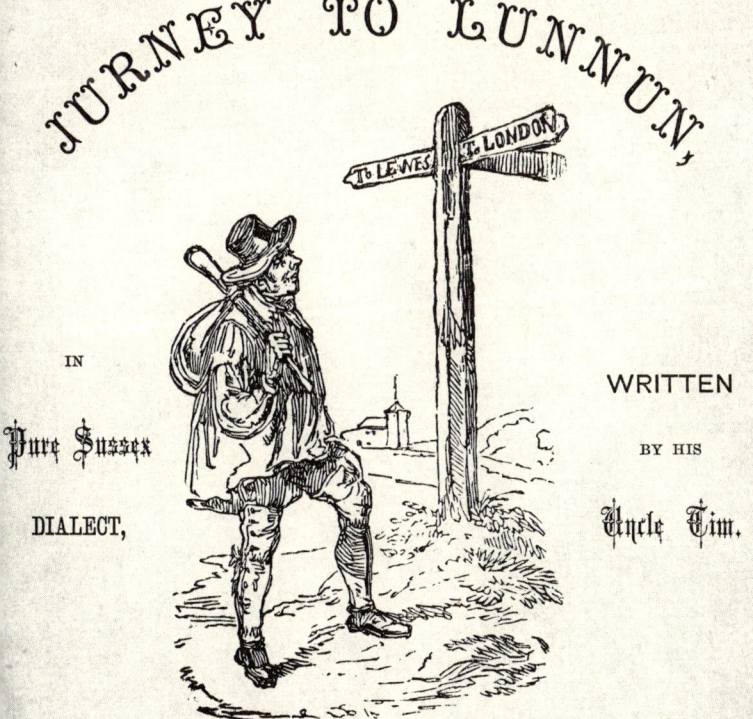

IN **𝔓𝔲𝔯𝔢 𝔖𝔲𝔰𝔰𝔢𝔵** DIALECT,

WRITTEN BY HIS **𝔘𝔫𝔠𝔩𝔢 𝔗𝔦𝔪.**

AND

JAN CLADPOLE'S
TRIP TO 'MERRICUR.

LEWES: FARNCOMBE & CO., "EAST SUSSEX NEWS" WORKS.

LEWES:
PRINTED BY FARNCOMBE AND CO.